Railroad Museum of Pennsylvania

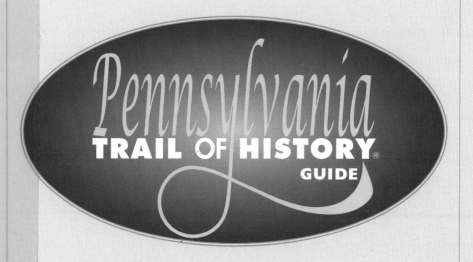

Text by Dan Cupper

STACKPOLE BOOKS

PENNSYLVANIA HISTORICAL
AND MUSEUM COMMISSION

Kyle R. Weaver, Series Editor
Tracy Patterson, Designer

Published by
STACKPOLE BOOKS
5067 Ritter Road
Mechanicsburg, Pennsylvania 17055

Pennsylvania Trail of History® is a registered trademark of the Pennsylvania Historical and Museum Commission.

Printed in the United States of America
2 4 6 8 10 9 7 5 3 1
FIRST EDITION

Maps by Caroline Stover

All photographs are from the collection of the Railroad Museum of Pennsylvania
Photographer credits are noted throughout

Steve Panopoulos: cover, 3, 5

Library of Congress Cataloging-in-Publication Data

Railroad Museum of Pennsylvania
    Railroad Museum of Pennsylvania: Pennsylvania trail of history guide / text by Dan Cupper.
        p. cm.—(Pennsylvania trail of history guides)
    Includes bibliographical references.
    ISBN 0-8117-2956-7
    1. Railroad Museum of Pennsylvania. 2. Railroad museums—Pennsylvania—Strasburg. I. Cupper, Dan. II. Title. III. Series.

TF6.U6 R35 2002
625.1'074'74815—dc21

2001049794

Contents

Editor's Preface

The Pennsylvania Historical and Museum Commission (PHMC) preserves the rich history of Pennsylvania's key industries in several museums it administers throughout the state. With this volume in the Pennsylvania Trail of History Guides, Stackpole Books is pleased to showcase the commission's remarkable collection of locomotives, railcars, and related artifacts and documents at the Railroad Museum of Pennsylvania.

The series, which profiles the historic sites and museums of the PHMC, was conceived and created by Stackpole Books with the cooperation of the PHMC's Division of Publications and Bureau of Historic Sites and Museums. Donna Williams heads the latter, and she and her staff of professionals review the text of each guidebook for historical accuracy and have made many valuable recommendations. Diane Reed, Chief of Publications, has facilitated relations between the PHMC and Stackpole from the project's inception, organized the review process with the commission, and attended to numerous details related to the venture.

For this volume, David Dunn, Director of the Railroad Museum of Pennsylvania, juggled a busy schedule to make time for several meetings with me to develop the project and sort through the museum's vast collection of photographs to illustrate the book. The contributions of his willing staff to the review process defy the cliché that too many cooks spoil the soup. Kurt Bell, Librarian/Archivist for the museum, helped in the photo selection, provided the author with important source material, and contributed an insightful review of the manuscript.

Dan Cupper, who wrote the text, is a transportation historian descended from a family of railroaders. He has written about Pennsylvania railroads in several articles and in his books *Horseshoe Heritage: The Story of a Great Railroad Landmark* and *Crossroads of Commerce: The Pennsylvania Railroad Calendar Art of Grif Teller*. He brings his specialized knowledge to this guidebook, offering a brief history of the railroad in Pennsylvania, the story of the museum that houses the industry's precious remnants, and a look at the facility and its extensive collection of rolling stock.

Kyle R. Weaver, Editor
Stackpole Books

No state has been more closely tied to the history, technology, and culture of railroading than Pennsylvania. For close to two hundred years, trains have been running here in one form or another, from the earliest crude, horse-drawn wooden guideway built by Thomas Leiper to serve a Delaware County quarry in 1809 to today's high-speed electric passenger trains and six-thousand-horsepower freight locomotives. Each year, 150,000 people visit the Railroad Museum of Pennsylvania to hear and experience the story.

When it was opened in 1975, the Railroad Museum of Pennsylvania was the first building in North America to be designed and built specifically as a railroad museum, not converted from an existing structure. The site today includes an outdoor restoration yard, several exhibit areas, dozens of locomotives and cars, a re-created 1910-era train station, an education center, an art gallery, a restoration shop, and a research center. In its collections, the museum preserves objects of the past to tell how railroading shaped—and was shaped by—the lives of those who worked for, rode on, lived near, admired, and invested in the railroads of the Keystone State. It is a tale about trains, but it is also a story of railroad people.

Railroading in Pennsylvania

Railroads helped Pennsylvania grow into a mining and manufacturing giant, and those industries helped the railroads grow by giving them business to handle. Because they could cheaply and rapidly carry goods and people through a mountainous terrain, railroads quickly replaced canals as the primary mode of Pennsylvania travel and shipping.

Working for the railroad often tended to be a family tradition. It wasn't unusual for several brothers, and sometimes sisters, to follow their father into a career in railroading. These were the men and women who worked aboard the trains and in the shops and stations, and maintained the track and signal systems. They took pride in working cooperatively to accomplish something much greater than themselves in an industry that, for a century, symbolized the industrial might of America.

The earliest trains were powered by horses and mules. Among the first was Thomas Leiper's three-quarter-mile-long wooden tramway railroad in Delaware County, Pennsylvania, built in 1809–10 to link a quarry with a boat landing.

CANALS AND EARLY RAILROADS

Some important early Pennsylvania railroads began as offshoots of canal companies. One in the northeastern part of the state, based at Honesdale, was the Delaware & Hudson Canal Company, which shipped barges of anthracite coal to New York City for home heating. The same company operated a gravity railroad—where loaded cars moved downhill by their own weight—and tried out the English-built Stourbridge Lion on August 8, 1829. Its seven-ton weight, combined with its power, was too much for the primitive and lightly constructed tracks, and the engine made only one more trip before being stored. But it was significant for being the first full-size steam locomotive to operate on a commercial railroad track in the United States. By 1830, the young nation counted a grand total of some twenty-three miles of railroad track.

On November 23, 1832, Old Ironsides, the first locomotive built by a predecessor of the Baldwin Locomotive Works, made a successful trial run on the Philadelphia, Germantown & Norristown Railroad. Baldwin eventually became the largest U.S. builder of steam locomotives. By that same year, forty-

The Railroad ushered in an era of industrial might for Pennsylvania. STEVE PANOPOULOS

were hanged, ten of them on a single day, June 21, 1877.

Other promoters had their eyes on the West, which at that time was defined as Cincinnati and New Orleans, reached via Pittsburgh through navigation on the Ohio and Mississippi Rivers. The state's joint canal-and-rail passage was inconvenient, inefficient, and dangerous. Trains didn't run at night, the canals froze in winter, and cables on the inclined planes sometimes snapped.

Philadelphia and Pittsburgh investors put up the money to build an all-rail route between the two cities. When the Pennsylvania Railroad (PRR) opened the Horseshoe Curve in 1854, its trains cut the travel time from three and a half days to just thirteen hours.

It was that railroad's president, J. Edgar Thomson (term, 1852–74), whose vision of expansion transformed the Philadelphia-based PRR from a local line into the nation's largest and most influential railroad, with twenty-six thousand miles of track and 280,000 employees by 1920. By 1874, just twenty years after the first train crossed the state, the system and its controlled subsidiaries reached from New York, Philadelphia, Baltimore, and Washington in the east to Chicago, St. Louis, Cleveland, Cincinnati, Indianapolis, and Louisville in the west. Within Pennsylvania, PRR penetrated fifty-five of the sixty-seven counties and reached every important city except Scranton, Allentown, and Bethlehem.

seven railroads had been chartered in Pennsylvania; of those, twenty-four were actually built.

During the 1830s, one of Pennsylvania's most important early freight-hauling railroads got its start—the Philadelphia & Reading, whose name was later shortened to Reading Company. On January 10, 1842, the line was completed for its ninety-four-mile original length from Philadelphia to Reading and on to Mount Carbon (near Pottsville), in the hard coal region. Eventually the Reading and its allies grew to link the coalfields with New York, becoming a powerful corporation whose economic reach was unmatched in the lower anthracite coal fields. It owned many of the mines it served, and employed a much-feared private constabulary, the coal and iron police. The Reading's president, Franklin B. Gowen, personally took on the task of presenting the prosecution case against members of a secret and violent Irish-American miners' group known as the Molly Maguires. Convicted of murdering P&R coal company superintendents, twenty of them

Thomson was driven by the conviction that the railroad that moved first to control outlets to the Midwest would prosper the most. He was not alone in holding that view. Eventually, the Baltimore & Ohio reached Pittsburgh in its quest to link Baltimore and Washington with Chicago. Also, the Erie, the Lake Shore & Michigan Southern (New York Central), and the Nickel Plate Road (New York, Chicago & St. Louis) Railroads also connected the East with Chicago, all by traversing the northwest corner of the state.

THE CIVIL WAR AND POSTWAR ERA

The Civil War was the first armed conflict in which railroads were militarily important, and the PRR and its allies profited handsomely by serving as a conduit for transporting, supplying, and redeploying Union troops and materiel. The Baltimore & Ohio, whose main line was situated much closer to the Mason-Dixon line than that of PRR, generally took the brunt of Confederate sabotage.

Townspeople of Columbia, Pennsylvania, however, burned the PRR-controlled railroad bridge over the Susquehanna River to prevent an invasion by approaching Rebels.

Herman Haupt, a West Point–trained civil engineer and bridge expert, was PRR's chief engineer from 1853 to 1856. During the Civil War, he went to work for the federal government, rebuilding war-damaged trestles. He rebuilt one bridge in fifteen hours. Another bridge, stretching four-hundred feet long and eighty feet high, was restored in nine days. President Lincoln later said, "[T]hat man Haupt has built a bridge across Potomac Creek . . . over which loaded trains are running every hour and, upon my word, gentlemen, there is nothing in it but beanpoles and cornstalks." Using his organizational skills to wring remarkable performance out of primitive equipment, Haupt also directed the repair and operation of railroads in Virginia, Maryland, and Pennsylvania, by which Union troops were

The Civil War. As a quick means for supplying and transporting troops, the railroad played a vital role during the conflict. Pennsylvania served as a crossroads for much of this activity.

resupplied. This included the Northern Central and Western Maryland lines in southcentral Pennsylvania, which he operated in July 1863 to support the Union Army at Gettysburg. In the end, the superiority of the rail network in the North was one of the factors that enabled the Union to win the war.

In the post–Civil War era, existing railroads continued to expand, and new ones were chartered almost daily. Nationally, railroad mileage jumped from 23 in 1830, to 30,000 in 1860, to nearly 160,000 by 1890. In Pennsylvania, the reasons for this boom were the rise of the iron and steel industries to fuel the nation's industrialization, the growth of both anthracite and bituminous coal mining, the rise of the lumber industry to meet burgeoning needs for housing, and the discovery of oil near Titusville. In the frenzy, scores of promoters' proposed, or "paper," railroads were devised but never built.

The biggest and best-known railroads were the major trunk lines, but connecting feeder lines played an important role as well. Independent short lines were built to serve the communities that lay from as little as five miles to perhaps fifty or sixty miles off the main lines. Often, these railroads were the only gateway from a county seat to the outside world,

and Pennsylvania boasted more short lines than any other state. Because they were financed and operated locally, most of them took on a distinct character and autonomous air that was undisturbed by corporate directives from some distant headquarters. Among these lines was the colorfully nicknamed "Ma & Pa," or Maryland & Pennsylvania, which linked rural York County with Baltimore. Short lines carried everything that trunk lines did, just not as much of it.

A specialized form of short line was the logging railroad, which lumber companies built into forests while they harvested timber. Usually privately owned and not common carriers—that is, not open to the public trade and not exchanging cars with the general railroad network—they were hastily laid up mountainsides and down hollows, with steep grades, sharp curves, and spindly trestles. The lines lasted no longer than it took to clear the wood from an area; the rails were pulled up and redeployed to the next stand of timber.

Standard-gauge track—a distance of four feet eight and one-half inches between the rails—slowly began to emerge as a uniform North American standard after the Civil War, as the tide of interstate commerce—and the importance of freely moving freight around the country without reloading cars at each junction—became clear. Even then, however, many short lines were built to narrow or nonstandard track gauge, usually three feet. Pennsylvania was home to many narrow-gauge railroads.

THE RAILROADING STATE

Pennsylvania stands tall in railroad history for many reasons:

• The first full-size steam locomotive to be operated in America ran at Honesdale on August 8, 1829.

• The world's largest commercial steam locomotive manufacturer, Baldwin Locomotive Works, began in Philadelphia as an offshoot of a watchmaker's trade. It produced steam, diesel-electric, and electric locomotives for 125 years.

• The world's most successful diesel-electric locomotive manufacturer, General Electric, is based in Erie and Grove City.

• Many railroad-supply firms settled here, among them, makers of steel rail, wheels, signals, air brakes, couplers, boiler staybolts, and coal stokers, as well as commercial builders of complete steam, diesel, and electric locomotives and freight and passenger cars.

• All four of the major trunk lines that connected the East Coast with Chicago passed through the state—the New York Central, Erie, Pennsylvania, and Baltimore & Ohio Railroads. These four not only aided in the westward settlement of the nation, but also served as the thread by which European immigrants found their destinies in the New World.

• During the height of travel by rail, passengers could board some of the nation's most exclusive passenger trains here, including the Broadway Limited and Capitol Limited (both New York–Chicago via different routes) and the Congressional and Royal Blue (New York–Philadelphia–Washington).

• Labor history was made in Pittsburgh with the railroad riots of 1877.

• The Pennsylvania Railroad shops at Altoona, employing 16,500 workers at their peak about 1916, once formed the largest such complex in the world.

• In the 1930s, Pennsylvania was a hub for the most successful mainline railroad electrification project in America—the Pennsylvania Railroad's New York–Washington and Philadelphia–Harrisburg routes. It is still in use today by Amtrak.

• Among the state's engineering landmarks are the Horseshoe Curve near Altoona, the stone-arch Rockville Bridge near Harrisburg, the concrete Tunkhannock Viaduct and stone-arch Starrucca Viaduct north of Scranton, and the Kinzua Viaduct near Kane.

• In the 1960s, Pennsylvania took an early lead in tourist railroad and railroad museum development.

The Horseshoe Curve, near Altoona.

Such lines were attractive because a railroad could be built for less initial capital cost, since everything about it was smaller—its grading, track, bridges, tunnels, and rolling stock. Two drawbacks, which eventually killed most of them, were that they had to pay competitive wages, and that they were incompatible with the rest of the North American rail network. The latter was not a problem as long as shipments remained local, but because narrow-gauge cars could not run on standard-gauge tracks, any freight going from one to the other had to be transferred by hand, raising labor costs and delaying the shipment.

Two Pennsylvania railroads that had somewhat the opposite problem, but the same drawbacks, were the Erie and the Delaware, Lackawanna & Western, both of which were built with a broad gauge (six feet between the rails) before a universal standard was adopted. They, and other broad-gauge lines, were built that way in the belief that a wider track made for greater stability. (Most lines in

the South were built to a five-foot gauge, and most Canadian railroads used a five-foot, six-inch gauge.) Both the Erie and the DL&W recognized that the ability to freely exchange cars was necessary to survive in an increasingly national economy, and both converted to standard gauge.

TECHNOLOGY AND SAFETY

In its first century, railroading was always a highly dangerous occupation. Human error and mechanical failures caused many accidents, serious injuries, and hundreds of fatalities among workers. Locomotive boilers exploded, hand brakes failed, axles broke, and journal bearings overheated and burned off. Runaways and derailments were everyday occurrences. Even more common were accidents during switching maneuvers, when brakemen had to step between cars to manually couple or uncouple them. Many men were crushed between cars during these operations, or their fingers were amputated when they

Track Gauge. Before a standard gauge for tracks was developed, the Erie Railroad, left, was laid in a broad, six-foot gauge. Many short line railroads in Pennsylvania established less-expensive narrow gauge tracks, usually three feet. The dual-gauge yard on the East Broadtop Railroad in Mount Union, Pennsylvania, right, shows a narrow track of three feet inside a standard track of four feet and eight and one-half inches.

tried to align the primitive link-and-pin couplers then in use.

Because the work was so hazardous, many insurance companies refused to write policies on the men who worked aboard the trains, so they formed their own benevolent mutual insurance brotherhoods, which became the basis from which locomotive and trainmen's unions sprang.

As trains got longer and heavier, and as locomotives to pull them got larger, railroads needed better ways of controlling all that weight and power, especially on curving, mountainous tracks. Pittsburgh inventor George Westinghouse experimented with several prototypes for the air brake, and finally the Pennsylvania Railroad gave it a trial on its Pittsburgh–Steubenville, Ohio, local. It turned out to be successful. Soon railroads were adding air brakes and automatic safety knuckle couplers, developed and patented by Eli Janney in 1868, to passenger trains, but it took a federal law in 1893 to force them to equip all of their trains, freight and passenger, with these safety devices.

As trains grew heavier, the iron rails that supported them wore out more quickly or simply broke under the strain, causing derailments and added costs and delays. The domestic steel industry got a boost when railroads became an early customer: The first steel rails in America were installed on the Pennsylvania Railroad. Using the Bessemer process, the Cambria Iron Works (later part of Bethlehem Steel Corporation) rolled them in 1867 at its plant in Johnstown.

BOOM, DECLINE, AND REBIRTH

By the late 1860s, trains were not only growing heavier and faster, but also traveling farther than ever before. The first transcontinental railroad was completed in 1869, making the New York–Chicago

Coupling. The dangers in this operation are apparent, as brakemen were required to go between two railcars to join them with a link-and-pin apparatus.

lines that passed through Pennsylvania even more important as an outlet to and from the East Coast.

Railroads became the focus of labor unrest in 1877, when a trainmen's strike that started on the Baltimore & Ohio Railroad in Maryland spread to Pennsylvania, most notably at Pittsburgh. In June, rioters torched dozens of locomotives, hundreds of cars, and scores of buildings in the largest act of civil disobedience in American history up to that point.

In 1880, with thirty thousand employees and $400 million in capital, the Pennsylvania Railroad was the nation's largest corporation. It stood apart from many railroads of that era because it was professionally managed by engineers, who understood the science of transportation. Other railroads, notably the New York Central, Reading, Erie, and Union Pacific, were characterized by colorful and wealthy "robber baron" leaders who often used financial might and personal charisma to manipulate Wall Street. A public backlash against big business generally and railroads in particular prompted Congress in 1887 to pass the Interstate Commerce

The Rockville Bridge, built in 1902, crosses the Susquehanna River, near Harrisburg, and is the longest stone-arch railroad bridge in the world. The locomotive in this view is a Pennsylvania Railroad M1.

Act, which set the stage for government regulation of the industry.

The late nineteenth and early twentieth century saw major expansion of both Pennsylvania's and America's railroads. Many railroad landmarks were constructed in the state during this period, such as the 301-foot-high Kinzua Viaduct near Kane (1882, rebuilt in 1900); Reading Terminal in Philadelphia (1893); Rockville Bridge near Harrisburg, the world's longest stone-arch railroad bridge (1902); and the concrete Tunkhannock Viaduct north of Scranton (1915). Railroad mileage in the state reached its peak of 11,500 miles in 1915.

Railroads became functionally and financially intertwined with the other large, heavy, labor-intensive industries of the day. Many carriers owned coal mines, among them the Pennsylvania, Reading, Lackawanna, Lehigh Valley, and Lehigh & New England Railroads. A few railroads owned heavy investments in steel mills. The Pennsylvania, for example, held an interest in the Pennsylvania Steel Company (later Bethlehem Steel) as a way to ensure a source of steel rails for itself. These relationships ended when public and Congressional fears of monopolies led to the passage in 1906 of the Hepburn Act, which made it illegal for railroads to carry goods in which they held a financial interest. Some common-ownership situations—in which steel companies owned railroads that served them—were untouched by the law. Bethlehem Steel owned common-carrier lines that served or fed raw materials to its mills, such as the Cambria & Indiana, Conemaugh & Black Lick, Steelton & Highspire, and Philadelphia, Bethlehem & New England Railroads. The United States Steel Corporation also owned many railroads that carried raw materials to its plants, including, in Pennsylvania, the Bessemer & Lake Erie, Union, and Johnstown & Stony Creek Railroads.

Women had always worked for railroads in office positions and as coach cleaners and telegraphers, but when men went off to fight in World War I, women took over some traditional male jobs such as track workers and crane operators, and this occurred even more during World War II.

Running a railroad was a vast and complex undertaking, requiring extraordinary communication and discipline. Workers were organized like an army and controlled by time schedules and rule books.

In the early twentieth century, railroads remained the primary means of travel and shipping. But soon the invention of the automobile and its cousins, the bus and the truck, had sparked a public demand for good roads. The completion of the Pennsylvania link in the coast-to-coast Lincoln Highway, America's first transcontinental road, started in 1913, opened the first crack in what had been the railroads' monopolistic armor. The coming of federal and state funding for highways started a long period of economic decline for railroads everywhere.

As the expansion of tracks into new areas ended, railroads turned to making improvements in technology and amenities. The first air-conditioned passenger car in America, a diner named Martha Washington, appeared on B&O trains running through Pennsylvania in 1931. Streamlined passenger trains appeared on the Reading and B&O lines soon thereafter. Many sleek streamliners built for railroads all over the United States were constructed by the Budd Company in Philadelphia, helping revive the sagging passenger business in the midst of the Great Depression.

World War II tested the railroads as never before, as they carried immense tonnage and millions of passengers,

Baldwin Locomotive Works, 1942.

Mrs. Casey Jones. During the World Wars, women worked the railroads, replacing the men who had been called to action. Mrs. Casey Jones was the female recruiting character for the Pennsylvania Railroad during World War II.

many of them soldiers on troop trains. Although the war did not reach American soil, railroads were considered to be such a strategic asset to winning an Allied victory that sentries were assigned to guard key bridges, tunnels, and stations against sabotage. The military importance of railroading was apparent in no place more than Pennsylvania, as main lines pulsed with troop trains and war materiel heading to or from East Coast ports, and trains bulged with coal, steel, and oil to support the Allied war effort.

Diesel locomotives made their debut in the late 1930s and early 1940s, and by 1957, most railroads had converted to them. Some steam-engine builders, such as Baldwin at Philadelphia, tried unsuccessfully to make the transition to building diesels and shut down. The workforce at the Altoona shops of the Pennsylvania Railroad, which had built more than sixty-five hundred steam engines since the 1860s, was decimated by thousands of layoffs when PRR

General Electric Locomotive Plant.

stopped new locomotive construction in 1946 and cut back to performing diesel maintenance and car construction and repair. The General Electric locomotive plant at Erie began building diesel road locomotives in 1959 and, by the 1990s, had become the dominant locomotive builder in North America.

As postwar America took to the highways, intercity passenger trains entered a period of long decline. Many American railroads began to lose money, especially in the Northeast. Crossing northwestern Pennsylvania, the Pittsburg, Shawmut & Northern Railroad had gone out of business in 1947, perhaps not notable, except for the fact that this was no short line—it was a two-hundred-mile-long railroad. The abandonment of such a large regional carrier was only the beginning of the bad news for Pennsylvania's railroad industry.

In 1956, after building more than seventy-five thousand steam, diesel, and electric locomotives in the Philadelphia area since 1831, Baldwin-Lima-Hamilton Corporation (formerly Baldwin Locomotive Works) turned out its final engine and exited the business. Baldwin was once the world's largest locomotive builder and a major exporter. The next year, the last train station to be built in Pennsylvania by a major private railroad was completed when B&O opened a modest commuter depot at 10 Grant Street in Pittsburgh.

Two of the best-known public icons of railroading—steam locomotives and passenger trains—began to disappear at a rapid rate. The Pennsylvania Railroad closed out its main-line steam operations in 1957. The success of the Pennsylvania Turnpike, the first superhighway in America, and other turnpikes triggered legislation to create a free interstate highway system, which was enacted into law in 1956. Rail passenger service began to erode, first on the branch lines and then on the main lines. Soon passenger trains on Harrisburg–Erie, Pittsburgh–Buffalo, and New York–Allentown–Wilkes-Barre–Buffalo routes made their last runs.

The coming of commercial jet travel in 1958 helped accelerate the railroads' demise. In 1961, the Lehigh Valley Railroad became one of the first major railroads in the nation to adopt a freight-only status when it discontinued its Black Diamond train, which had run between New York and Buffalo via Bethlehem, Allentown, Lehighton, and Wilkes-Barre. Local service was in trouble too. Regional government bodies such as the Southeastern Pennsylvania Transportation Authority (SEPTA) were created to take over failing commuter service as an alternative to building additional highways, which were becoming ever more crowded. Freight lines were also struggling. The New York, Ontario, & Western Railroad, in 1957, became the first Class 1 railroad to completely abandon operations in Pennsylvania.

In their fight to survive, most of Pennsylvania's railroads forgot about the public and their own rich heritage, and focused almost wholly on serving their freight shippers. One exception was the Reading Company, which from 1959 to 1964 revived several of its T-1 class 4-8-4 steam locomotives, all of which had been built at the carrier's locomotive shops in Reading, and mounted dozens of the immensely popular "Iron Horse Rambles," excursions throughout eastern Pennsylvania. They operated to or through Philadelphia, Coatesville, Pottstown, Schwenksville, Reading, Allentown, Bethlehem, Tamaqua, Shamokin, Sunbury, Williamsport, Harrisburg, Hershey, and Gettysburg, as well as on lines running into New Jersey and Delaware.

Economic disadvantages, such as large yard and terminal costs, the inability to afford labor-saving innovations, overgenerous union contracts, and passenger operations, burdened nearly all of the major trunk lines that operated in Pennsylvania, driving many of them to bankruptcy or its brink in the 1960s and 1970s. The Penn Central, Erie Lackawanna, Reading, Jersey Central, Lehigh Valley, and Lehigh & Hudson River Railroads all went bankrupt, and the Baltimore & Ohio was nearly so. All were major players in Pennsylvania.

The crisis prompted the federal government to step in to preserve essential freight and passenger service. Congress passed legislation creating two new corporations: Amtrak, formed May 1, 1971, to take over intercity rail passenger service, and Conrail, formed April 1, 1976, for northeastern freight service. Amtrak has continued to advance railroading technology by bringing high-speed (150 mph) rail service to the Northeast Corridor in an effort to stay competitive with air travel. Conrail took over the bankrupt remains of Penn Central, Erie Lackawanna, Reading, Lehigh Valley, and others. Congressional regulatory reforms placed railroads on a more level playing field with other modes of transportation, finally loosening the shackles that came in the wake of the Interstate Commerce Act of 1887. Conrail succeeded in turning around the fortunes of northeastern freight railroading and became profitable. Its key location made it a desirable plum for other eastern carriers, and in 1999 it was split up and sold to CSX Transportation and Norfolk Southern Railroad.

In the midst of all of this, something occurred to show that Americans had not totally lost their fascination with trains. In 1975 and 1976, the American Freedom Train, carrying national icons and documents, made a coast-to-coast tour to celebrate the bicentennial of American independence. The train made multiday stops along the way for paying visitors, with Pennsylvania sites including King of Prussia, Bethlehem, Scranton, Harrisburg, Williamsport, Brackenridge, and Pittsburgh. It also passed through Gettysburg and York, and stopped to pose for a photograph on the Horseshoe Curve. On its eastern leg, the twenty-five-car train was powered by former Reading Company T-1 steam engine No. 2102, one of the stars of the old Iron Horse Rambles. Aboard were more than five hundred artifacts, including the Bill of Rights, the Louisiana Purchase, Judy Garland's dress from the film *The Wizard of Oz*, Joe Frazier's boxing trunks, President Abraham Lincoln's stovepipe hat, and a moon rock. On its two-year journey, seven million people waited hours in line to board the train, and many more lined the tracks to watch it steam past. It proved that Americans still loved trains, even if they didn't ride them much anymore.

History of the Railroad Museum of Pennsylvania

When a group of historians organized for the first time specifically to study American railroad heritage, the industry was already mature. Railroading had been around for a century before the formation of the Railway & Locomotive Historical Society in 1921. R&LHS was followed by the National Railway Historical Society, founded in 1935 in Lancaster, Pennsylvania. NRHS eventually became the largest railroad-enthusiast group in North America, growing to embrace more than 175 chapters and some twenty thousand members. Pennsylvania is home to more of those chapters than any other state. Remaining one of the most active in the society, the Lancaster Chapter has supported the Railroad Museum of Pennsylvania, cosponsored many programs and projects with it, and restored and donated equipment to it. The emergence of such enthusiast groups in the 1930s was an early gauge of the popular sentiment that would lead to creation of this and other railroad museums.

Through the 1930s, railroad enthusiast clubs began to charter trains over rural and little-seen routes, which abounded—and still abound—in Pennsylvania. Sponsoring and riding on these excursions encouraged a sense of camaraderie and identity. Still the dominant mode of travel and shipping, railroads viewed themselves as institutions with a public face and public responsibilities. As such, they conducted many special public events and displays of equipment, either on their own or in conjunction with other widely attended festivities. For example, the Pennsylvania, Baltimore & Ohio, and Western Maryland Railroads often displayed locomotives and cars at the York Inter-State Fair, an annual end-of-summer agricultural gathering in York County with roots that extend back to the 1760s. The Pennsylvania Railroad, dominant railroad of the state and the Northeast, also often parked its latest equipment in walk-through displays at the state Farm Show in Harrisburg, held each January.

The Pennsylvania Railroad had recognized the historical significance of the technology early on, donating the original 1831 John Bull steam engine to the Smithsonian Institution in 1885 and setting aside a few other vintage pieces. Over the years, the company also gathered, at its headquarters in Philadelphia's Broad Street Station, other early

George M. Hart Locomotive and Rolling Stock Hall in the Railroad Museum of Pennsylvania. STEVE PANOPOULOS

New York World's Fair, 1939–40. The railroads proudly exhibited their progress by featuring the newest, state-of-the-art models beside equipment from the past.

artifacts, including pieces of rail, photographs, newspaper clippings, timetables, tickets, stock certificates, tools, books, and other hardware, forming a sort of informal private museum.

The PRR's change from wooden to steel freight and passenger cars accelerated after 1910, and many older pieces that might have been candidates for preservation were simply dismantled or their wooden bodies burned, after any reusable metal parts were scavenged from the carcasses. The 1930s brought a general purge of active older steam locomotives when the Pennsy pushed forward its massive program to electrify its eastern main lines. With the arrival of electric locomotives on PRR routes between New York, Philadelphia, Baltimore, and Washington, and between Philadelphia and Harrisburg, hundreds of newer steam engines that once worked in that region were redeployed across the rest of the system, and older ones were scrapped.

For what became the most ambitious of all such exhibitions, PRR and all of the other major eastern railroads sponsored a mammoth railroad-industry pavilion at the 1939–40 New York World's Fair. Not only did they use this as a showcase for their newest locomotives and cars, but they also restored old equipment for display and operation. A Broadway-like living-history pageant with moving trains, old and new, called "Railroads on Parade," highlighted the central role of railroads in building and settling the United States.

This required old engines and cars, with actors representing crew members and passengers wearing period costumes, but PRR no longer had any truly old or historic locomotives tucked away in storage. John Bull was at the Smithsonian, the 1851 locomotive Pioneer had been loaned by the PRR for display at the Franklin Institute in Philadelphia, and the 1868 locomotive Reuben Wells had been donated to Purdue University. The purges of the 1930s had eliminated most others. In 1933, the PRR had donated its first John Stevens replica, built in its Altoona Shops in 1928, to the Chicago Museum of Science and Industry.

But a search of industries to which the PRR had sold older engines for secondhand use turned up an 1888 freight locomotive still working at a quarry in Birdsboro, Pennsylvania. PRR traded a more modern switching engine that was surplus to the quarry company and sent the old engine, former PRR No. 1187, a 2-8-0 type, back to its shops in Altoona, where it was restored. The Altoona shops also restored some old wooden coaches and, in the most amazing step of all, constructed a brand new full-size reproduction of the John Bull for the second year of the fair.

After the fair, PRR moved its older pieces into storage at roundhouses in Wilmington, Delaware; East Trenton, New Jersey; and Northumberland, Pennsylvania. (By the mid-1950s, all PRR Historic Collection pieces were consolidated at Northumberland.) Many years later, that collection became the centerpiece of the Railroad Museum of Pennsylvania. Many historians now consider the "Railroads on Parade" exhibit at the fair to be the high-water mark of public railroad pageantry.

In November 1940, the identity of enthusiasts became even more solidified with the appearance of a new popular magazine titled *Trains*, the first American periodical specifically aimed at railroad enthusiasts and historians.

From 1947 through 1950, several special trains traveled around the state, stopping to visit major towns. Among them were the first Freedom Train, carrying national historic treasures for public display, and the Friendship Train, carrying food for starving postwar Europe. A "Pennsylvania Week" train, with engines and cars contributed by all of the state's major railroads, traveled from town to town, promoting Pennsylvania business, industry, and tourism.

The Chicago Railroad Fair of 1948–49 capitalized on the public fascination with railroads and railroading history. On display there was a fast passenger locomotive from 1902, No. 8063, which PRR had restored to resemble the engine No. 7002 that had pulled the New York–Chicago Pennsylvania Special on a leg of its speedy inaugural run on June 11, 1905. The original engine had been scrapped in 1934, so PRR took this similar but not identical survivor, overhauled it, repainted it, and gave it the number of the more famous locomotive.

Also in the late 1940s, the Association of American Railroads began to sponsor a national "Railroad Hour" radio broadcast. Still more signs of public interest began to appear. The National Museum of Transport was established in 1944 in St. Louis, Missouri. And in 1953, the Baltimore & Ohio Railroad opened a major railroad museum in its Mount Clare shops, a few blocks from downtown Baltimore.

In 1947, PRR management had made the final decision to drop steam power in favor of diesel-electric locomotives for its nonelectrified lines. The scrapping of thousands of steam engines began, but a few railroad officials set aside one example of each of the notable classes of PRR steam engines. Most were gathered up and sent for storage to a roundhouse at Northumberland on PRR's Harrisburg–Buffalo line. Eventually the list of preserved locomotives included two switching locomotives; five passenger locomotives; seven freight locomotives; the 1940 John Bull reproduction; two nineteenth-century engines from predecessor lines that had been returned from their borrowers, the Pioneer (1851) and Reuben Wells (1868); several wooden and early steel passenger cars; an 1888 tool car; and an early wooden Cumberland Valley Railroad combination baggage-coach car.

Aside from the fact that these officials recognized the importance of preserving technology, it appears that they had no clear thought in mind about what to do with the collection of engines. With the end of PRR's steam-locomotive operations in 1957, the roundhouse at Northumberland ceased to maintain active steam engines, and its

JOHN BULL

The story of the twin John Bull locomotives—the restored 1831 original in the Smithsonian Institution and the working 1940 reproduction in the Railroad Museum of Pennsylvania—explains how the core of the museum's collection got its start.

John Bull had been built in Newcastle-on-Tyne, England, disassembled, and shipped across the Atlantic in kit form. It was reassembled in New Jersey for use on a predecessor of the Pennsylvania Railroad, the Camden & Amboy Railroad, under the watchful eye of C&A master mechanic Isaac Dripps. It was first steamed up in November 1831 in Bordentown, New Jersey, and began regular service in 1833. The C&A fitted the John Bull with lead wheels and a cowcatcher—the first time these devices were used.

After a career of hauling local passengers and, later, gravel and work trains, the locomotive was recognized to be a relic as early as 1858, when it was exhibited at the New Jersey State Agricultural Fair. It was retired in 1866, but someone took note of its historical significance as one of the oldest surviving steam locomotives in America and stored it rather than selling it for secondhand use or scrap.

In 1871, the Pennsylvania Railroad gained control of the Camden & Amboy, and a few years later began to ponder how it would celebrate the national centennial anniversary of the nation's birth. Both the young republic and the PRR were born in Philadelphia. Though the nation's capital had moved to Washington, the railroad's headquarters were still located in Philadelphia, where the celebration would be held. For the occasion, the railroad pulled out the John Bull and began to "restore" it, though not always with the keenest eye to accuracy. It was displayed at the United States Centennial Exposition in Philadelphia in 1876, and again at a railway supply trade show in Chicago in 1883.

PRR donated the locomotive to the Smithsonian Institution in 1885. A few years later, the museum loaned the engine back to the PRR to make its longest run—more than nine hundred miles. Operating under its own power, it traveled over the PRR main line from Jersey City via Philadelphia, Harrisburg, and Pittsburgh to Chicago for display at the 1893 World's Columbian Exposition. After the fair closed, it returned, again under its own power, and was placed on public view at the Smithsonian's Arts and Industries Building in Washington. Later, in 1927, it made a final appearance at the Baltimore & Ohio's Fair of the Iron Horse in Halethorpe, Maryland.

For the 1939–40 New York World's Fair, PRR's Altoona shops in May 1940 constructed a full-size working reproduction of the original

primary function became to house the historic collection. Occasionally the railroad pulled some of the pieces out for various displays, such as for local civic celebrations, groups of visiting railroad enthusiasts, or special events elsewhere on the PRR system.

Over time, PRR officials randomly separated certain single pieces of the collection and sent them off to various new homes—Pioneer and an 1836 Camden & Amboy wooden coach to the Smithsonian in Washington (1960); Reuben Wells and an 1888 Class TA tool car to a children's museum in Indianapolis (1968); heavy I1sa-class 2-10-0 freight locomotive No. 4483 to a display at the gate of Westinghouse Air Brake in Wilmerding, Pennsylvania, near Pittsburgh (1963); and former Waynesburg & Washington Railroad 2-6-0 narrow-gauge engine No. 4 to the Greene County Fairgrounds at Waynesburg, Pennsylvania, near where the engine had run in its working days (1958). Also, the first K4s-class 4-6-2 passenger engine, No. 1737, was so far deteriorated that PRR withdrew it from the collection and scrapped it, substituting a later engine of the same class, No. 3750, which it

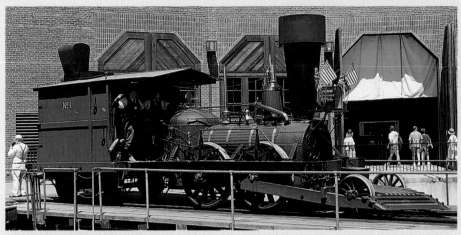

The 1940 John Bull on tour in Sacramento, California, 1999. EARL KINARD JR.

John Bull. The engine became part of the railroad's holdings of historic rolling stock, much of which went on long-term loan to the Railroad Museum of Pennsylvania after it was opened in 1975. In late 1979, special legislation enabled the museum to officially take title to that group of equipment, securing its future as the core of the rolling-stock collection.

With the ownership issue settled, museum staff and Strasburg Rail Road shop personnel noted the good mechanical condition of the John Bull reproduction and began restoring it. After months of work, it was returned to operating condition and for the first time in decades, it was steamed up on May 21, 1983.

A wood-burning locomotive, it still occasionally runs on the museum grounds and on the adjacent Strasburg Rail Road, and it has made appearances at California State Railroad Museum's Railfair in Sacramento; at Steamexpo in Vancouver, British Columbia; at Steamtown National Historic Site in Scranton, Pennsylvania; and at the Altoona Railroaders Memorial Museum in Altoona, Pennsylvania. In these ways, it continues to serve as an ambassador for the museum and for the profession of railroading as it was practiced in the earliest days of steam trains.

renumbered 1737 to represent the scrapped original.

PRESERVING RAILROAD HERITAGE

With the demise of the railroads in the face of growing competition from automobiles, trucks, and airplanes, enthusiasts and historians saw a need to begin preserving railroad heritage. As a result, here and there, concerned and committed historians began to take the first steps toward creating an independent railroad preservation and history field. One of the earliest examples was the group of rail fans and investors who

bought the failing Strasburg Rail Road (SRR) in Lancaster County in the fall of 1958. On January 4, 1959, after refurbishing the track on the four-and-a-half-mile-long route, they ran their first public excursion train over what was, and still is, the nation's oldest surviving short-line railroad. But the Strasburg Rail Road did not remain alone in the tourist-railroad business for long. Pennsylvania soon became a hub for steam locomotive preservation and operation. Within a few years, it boasted eight steam tourist railroads, more than any other state at the time. It was the even-

The Strasburg Rail Road *was revitalized as a tourist railroad by a group of enthusiasts in 1958. It remains today the oldest short-line railroad in the United States.*

tual success of the SRR that made Strasburg a candidate for the commonwealth's railroad museum.

Difficult times for the railroads forced many to consider merging to combine facilities, reduce workforces, and cut costs. In 1960, the first major railroad merger to affect Pennsylvania took place when the Erie Railroad and the Delaware, Lackawanna & Western Railroad joined to form Erie Lackawanna. Within the life span of one generation, such historic and colorful railroad names as Pennsylvania, New York Central, Nickel Plate Road, Reading, Lehigh Valley, Baltimore & Ohio, Jersey Central, and Pittsburgh & West Virginia would disappear in similar mergers. Each time a name or a corporate entity disappeared, it underscored the transitory nature of the railroad business, nudging historians to push for a permanent site to mark the state's railroad heritage.

In 1963, the chairman of the Pennsylvania Historical and Museum Commission (PHMC), James B. Stevenson, publisher of the *Titusville Herald* and a lifelong railroad buff, conceived the idea of a statewide railroad museum. At that time, the state was considering establishing a series of museums to highlight its significant industries, including lumber-

ing, agriculture, coal mining, ironmaking, and oil production, and the legislature authorized the creation of a railroad museum, to be known initially as the Pennsylvania Museum of Rail Transportation.

The following year, the PHMC began the site selection process. Three locales were considered: Altoona, Blair County, location of the Pennsylvania Railroad's sprawling systemwide shops complex and employer at its peak of 16,500 railroad-shop workers; Mount Union, Huntingdon County, site of the coal classification yard of the narrow-gauge East Broad Top Railroad, disused since the railroad had shut down in 1956, although EBT itself was revived in 1960 as a steam tourist railroad, with its original equipment, and the active portion of its line lay only about five miles south of Mount Union yard; and Strasburg, Lancaster County, home to the Strasburg Rail Road, by now well established as a thriving steam tourist line with a stable visitation base that was aided by its location in the heart of Pennsylvania Dutch country.

Meanwhile, the federal government had also begun recognizing the importance of railroad history in Pennsylvania, and that same year, 1964, the National Park Service established the Allegheny Portage Railroad National Historic Site near Cresson and designated the East Broad Top a National Historic Landmark. A few years later, the Horseshoe Curve near Altoona, an engineering landmark dating from 1854, was also designated a National Historic Landmark.

The PRR officially took a position favoring Altoona as the museum site but stopped short of offering to support it with a donation of land or vacant shop buildings, both of which it possessed in abundance. East Broad Top promised to give land for the museum and to reopen its line to Mount Union and extend its steam tourist operation to the site, thus providing a live steam presence. Strasburg held no historic ties to the railroad industry, as the other two did, but it was situated in the midst of a busy tourist area, while the other sites were relatively isolated from the state's large cities. Mount Union had the advantage of an active steam railroad, but at Altoona, the Pennsylvania Railroad was in no way interested in operating steam service. Had the PHMC located the museum at Altoona, the state would have had to get into the steam railroad business directly, which it did not want to do.

In a tight four-to-three vote on February 18, 1965, the PHMC commissioners selected Strasburg. The vote was controversial, because the location could not even remotely be considered a historic railroad site, as could so many other places in railroad-rich Pennsylvania. But it was situated next to an operating tourist railroad, where visitors could see and experience living steam engine technology as well as historical displays and interpretation. Perhaps relieved that it would not have to deal with the museum on its own turf in Altoona, PRR offered

The Train of Locomotives on the Strasburg Rail Road, en route to the new Railroad Museum, August 1969. WILLIAM M. MOEDINGER JR.

to donate some pieces from its historic collection housed at Northumberland.

CREATING THE MUSEUM

In June 1965, the museum purchased its first steam locomotive, a fifty-three-ton 1918 wood-burning Heisler Locomotive Works logging-company engine that had been built in Erie, Pennsylvania. Later that summer, on August 5, the Strasburg Rail Road steamed up a 1905 PRR D16sb-class 4-4-0 locomotive, No. 1223, which had been on display there since 1960 as a loan from PRR's Northumberland collection. For the next twenty-three years, including after it became the property of the museum, it served as a living-history link to the heritage of Pennsylvania Railroad steam engine technology. It was often used on special excursions, including many that ventured over the former PRR main line to Lancaster, Harrisburg, and Philadelphia.

In 1966, the legislature voted to provide $980,000 for planning and acquiring artifacts for the museum. A Pittsburgh architectural firm, Stotz, Hess & MacLachlan, began designing the structure. At the end of that year, the first steam locomotive to be donated to the museum was given by the Norfolk & Western Railway, the 220-ton former Nickel Plate Road 2-8-4 Berkshire-type fast-freight engine No. 757, which had been used between Chicago, Cleveland, Erie, and Buffalo.

Property acquisition began in 1967, with the state purchasing an initial seven-acre farmland site, later doubled

Nickel Plate Road No. 757, built in 1944, became the first steam locomotive donated to the Railroad Museum of Pennsylvania.

in size. The museum acquired by donation a former Reading Company hundred-foot-long turntable, from Luria Brothers Scrapyard, to serve as the visual and operational hub of its outdoor activities. Formerly used at West Cressona and later at Bridgeport, both in Pennsylvania, it was built by the American Bridge Company of Ambridge, Pennsylvania, in 1928; it arrived aboard three flatcars. Also in 1967, the PHMC officially dubbed the facility Railroad Museum of Pennsylvania. This phrasing carefully avoided any implication, as in Pennsylvania Railroad Museum, that the institution was part of the Pennsylvania Railroad or was intended to house relics from only that carrier.

Recognizing the heritage represented by the Baldwin Locomotive Works, the museum in 1968 bought an 1875 Mogul-type 2-6-0 locomotive for $20,000 from its California owner. Named Tahoe, the engine was built at Baldwin's plant in Philadelphia for the Virginia & Truckee Railroad in the silver-mining country of Nevada. Its acquisition was intended to highlight Baldwin's dominance in nineteenth-century locomotive manufacturing.

The year 1969 was an eventful one, with the laying of first track, the hiring of a director, and the arrival of the first promised pieces from the PRR collection. In June, George M. Hart was appointed director. A lifelong railroad historian from Doylestown, Bucks County, Hart owned several steam locomotives and a large fleet of passenger coaches, and was widely known for conducting occasional main-line and branch-line excursions with them. Four steam locomotives from the PRR Northumberland collection, which had been spruced up at Penn Central's Altoona shops, arrived at Strasburg on August 6. Most of the other pieces from that collection arrived two months later.

In 1970, ground was broken for the pit of the turntable. Plans called for seventeen display tracks to radiate from it. Meanwhile, the gathering of rolling stock moved forward with the acquisition of a streamlined passenger car from one of the state's best-known trains—the observation car Tower View from PRR's Broadway Limited (New York–Chicago via Philadelphia and Pittsburgh). The following year, the turntable was installed, and a fenced area became the first section of the museum to open to the public, on weekends only.

In 1971, Amtrak was formed, inheriting a rag-tag fleet of worn-out locomotives and cars from a variety of carriers and in widely varying conditions. As the railroad bought new equipment, it retired older pieces, and years later, several of them made their way into the museum's collection.

Although the museum in the early 1970s was busy arranging to acquire locomotives and cars, it also had its eye on other kinds of artifacts. In March 1972, at

THE LINDBERGH SPECIAL

In the early twentieth century, speed was what railroads were selling to the public. Many locomotives in the museum collection were fast passenger engines, but none of them gained more renown than Pennsylvania Railroad No. 460. When it raced an airplane one day in 1927, it earned the nickname "the Lindbergh engine."

After aviator Charles Lindbergh made his pioneer solo transatlantic New York–Paris flight in 1927, he returned to the United States aboard a navy cruiser that docked at Washington on June 11. In a triumphant ceremony, he was welcomed by President Calvin Coolidge and awarded the Congressional Medal of Honor. Cameramen recorded the event, and the newsreels were destined for New York City, where eager audiences would be waiting to see them in crowded theaters along Broadway. Several film companies hired planes to make the dash, but one competitor, the International News Reel Corporation, chartered a PRR train. The company outfitted a baggage car with a darkroom to process the film en route so that upon arrival, the newsreels could be delivered directly to theaters.

The engine chosen to handle the Lindbergh Special was No. 460, a PRR Class E6s 4-4-2 type engine built in August 1914 at the railroad's Altoona shops. Although larger and more powerful engines were available, the E6s type was swift, just right for a two-car train whose only mission was to race from Washington Union Station to New York in as little time as possible. A coach was added for a few PRR officials and assorted riders, but its role was mainly to provide additional braking power for the slowdowns from high speed.

Dispatchers cleared the tracks of other trains. As soon as the International couriers raced up the platform and deposited the film cans on the baggage car, the engineman yanked the throttle, pulling away at 12:14 P.M. After getting out of the yards, the engine surged ahead, accelerating to 95 MPH before slowing to pass through tunnels under the city of Baltimore. Once clear of the city, the engine again accelerated, at times reaching 110 MPH. At one point, a plane from a rival newsreel company dropped out of the sky and paced the train at 85 MPH, dipping its wings in salute, and then soaring away. After a brief water stop at Wilmington, Delaware, the Lindbergh Special continued on, hitting a reported 115 MPH. After slowing for Philadelphia, the train accelerated again, as back

The Lindbergh Special, No. 460, and Crew, 1927.

in the baggage car, darkroom technicians developed and dried the film, while an editor cut and spliced it into ten completed reels.

Near Princeton Junction, the Special reached 114 MPH before slowing for an S-curve at Elizabeth, New Jersey. East of Newark, the train stopped to change engines so that an electric locomotive could forward it the last few miles through the New York tunnels to Pennsylvania Station in Manhattan. When the train stopped there at 3:21 P.M., couriers grabbed the newsreels. Just fifteen minutes later, projectors started showing the films. The planes had actually reached New York first, but the strategy of processing en route had paid off. International's films were shown more than an hour ahead of those that had been flown. The race was essentially a harbinger of contemporary competition between Amtrak and the airline shuttles on the Northeast Corridor.

The Tahoe, built in 1875 by Baldwin Locomotive Works in Philadelphia, was an early acquisition for the museum and is one of the finest examples of nineteenth-century locomotive technology and design.

a four-day bankruptcy auction of the Penn Central's library and memorabilia holdings in Philadelphia, the museum emerged as the single largest buyer, spending more than $27,000 on photos, timetables, stock certificates, books, models, passes, atlases, and annual reports. This historic material formed the basis for the museum's renowned archival and library collections.

Groundbreaking ceremonies were held on August 14, 1972, for the museum's two-story main building and thirteen-hundred-foot-long rolling-stock hall. The museum opened on April 22, 1975. More than 7,300 people visited in the first week; and by year's end, 344,337 people had visited the site. The facility was the first state-owned railroad museum in the United States, the Nevada State Railroad Museum opening in 1980, the California State Railroad Museum main facility in 1981, and the North Carolina Museum of Transportation in 1983.

In the spring of 1976, the museum collecting policy widened when the institution acquired its first diesel locomotive, former Pennsylvania Railroad E7 type No. 5901, a two-thousand-horse-power streamlined passenger unit built in 1945 that was one of the first two

road diesel/electric locomotives bought by PRR. It was once used on the Red Arrow, Broadway Limited and other feature trains. Its preservation was assured when a roundhouse foreman at Harrisburg "hid" it from Penn Central officials, allowing it to escape the scrapper's torch. A few years earlier, in 1973, the museum had purchased its first electric locomotive, former Pennsylvania Railroad B1-class switcher No. 5690, formerly used in Sunnyside Yard in New York, Harrisburg, and other electrified areas.

But 1976 was also the year that Congress redrew the railroad map across the Northeast and Midwest, profoundly affecting the nature and physical reach of railroads in Pennsylvania. On April 1, several bankrupt lines—Penn Central, Reading, Lehigh Valley, Erie Lackawanna, Jersey Central, and Lehigh & Hudson River—were merged into the government-backed Consolidated Rail Corporation, or Conrail. As Penn Central had done earlier, Conrail kept its headquarters in Philadelphia.

Conrail eventually donated a number of pieces to the museum's rolling-stock collection. After the transition, nonoperating assets such as the former PRR historical collection remained in the hands of trustees of Penn Central. The next year, the museum hired consultants to appraise that collection, which was displayed at the museum but still owned by Penn Central Company. No longer a functioning railroad, Penn Central began to receive offers for individual pieces of the collection and considered splitting up the group and selling off items piecemeal. A frantic rush then began to work out a deal with

Penn Central, because a break-up of the collection to resolve tax indebtedness was a real possibility.

Special legislation was finally passed by the state House and Senate on December 31, 1979, authorizing the state to accept the former PRR historical collection in exchange for forgiveness of $1.2 million in back tax debt for Penn Central, thus eliminating the threat that the twenty-seven-piece group might be broken up and sold off.

Although many pieces that came to the museum were in poor condition and needed paint and restoration work, one already restored car was donated in 1981. It was a fully functional Pullman Company sleeper-restaurant-lounge car, built in 1913 and rebuilt in the 1930s, that had once been used in Pennsylvania on the Pittsburgh & Lake Erie Railroad.

In 1982, the Strasburg Rail Road leased a second member of the PRR historical collection, 4-4-2 steam engine No. 7002, for restoration to operating condition. After a long period of evaluation and reconditioning, it joined the museum's PRR No. 1223 in 1983 in regular tourist service. Both engines were used to pull special off-line excursions and for film and television-commercial use until 1990, when they were returned to the museum.

Recognizing the fact that rail fans and railroaders have allegiances to favorite railroads, just as sports fans prefer their favorite teams, the museum in 1984 held the first of what became annual events centered on the theme of a specific carrier: Reading Days for the Reading Railroad and Pennsy Days for the Pennsylvania. Featured during each are displays, artwork, model railroads, vendors, and illustrated lectures that focus on the particular railroad. The next year, 1985, the tenth year since the museum opened its doors, it welcomed its two millionth visitor.

Much of the collecting emphasis in the museum's early years reflected eastern Pennsylvania interests. To tell the story of western Pennsylvania railroading as well, the museum in 1992 sent a team to look for rolling-stock pieces that would help illustrate that segment of the railroad world, particularly items related to the steel industry. The result was the acquisition of a Monongahela Connecting Railroad Alco C-415 switching locomotive and a Pittsburgh & Lake Erie bay-window caboose, both of which had worked for steel-hauling railroads.

FRIENDS OF THE RAILROAD MUSEUM

A volunteer auxiliary organization to the museum was organized in January 1983 to provide a formal way to channel private-sector time, energy, and finances into the museum's mission. Called Friends of the Railroad Museum (FRM), its aim was to aid the state in operating the museum and in conserving, restoring, and interpreting its resources. Formation of the FRM was prompted by the deterioration of many locomotives and cars stored outdoors. FRM's energy is devoted to supplying volunteer and paid staff support, much of it targeted at reversing the weather decay on outdoor exhibits; conducting major fund-raising activities; and presenting educational programs on a variety of railroad-related subjects.

Restoration Crew. Part of the mission of the Friends of the Railroad Museum is to provide labor to restore locomotives and railcars.

Visiting the Museum

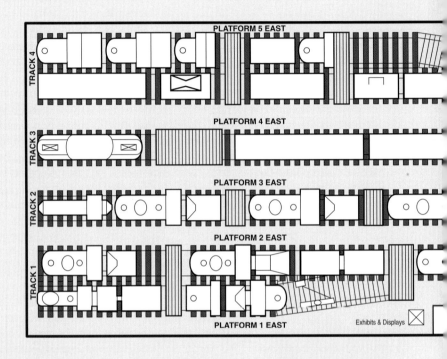

TRACK 4 — PLATFORM 5 EAST

TRACK 3 — PLATFORM 4 EAST

TRACK 2 — PLATFORM 3 EAST

PLATFORM 2 EAST

TRACK 1 — PLATFORM 1 EAST

Exhibits & Displays

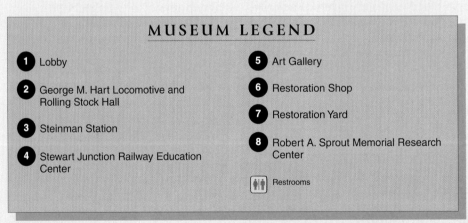

MUSEUM LEGEND

1 Lobby

2 George M. Hart Locomotive and Rolling Stock Hall

3 Steinman Station

4 Stewart Junction Railway Education Center

5 Art Gallery

6 Restoration Shop

7 Restoration Yard

8 Robert A. Sprout Memorial Research Center

Restrooms

1 LOBBY

A visit to the museum begins in the lobby, where one can buy admission, ask questions, and get directions to the exhibits. Adjacent to the Lobby is the Whistle Stop Shop, offering books, photos, memorabilia, postcards, puzzles, children's games, and other train-related items.

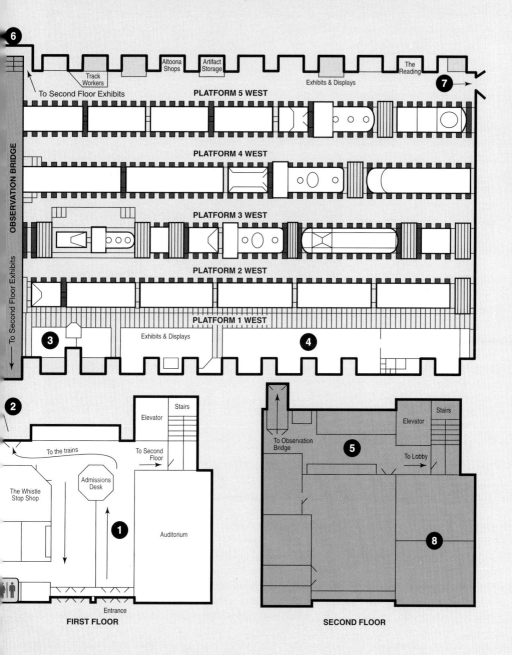

FIRST FLOOR

SECOND FLOOR

② GEORGE M. HART LOCOMOTIVE AND ROLLING STOCK HALL

From the Lobby, visitors enter the George M. Hart Locomotive and Rolling Stock Hall, named in honor of the museum's first director. Inside the Rolling Stock Hall are dozens of locomotives and cars, each telling a different chapter in the story of railroading in Pennsylvania. The more than one hundred items in the collection represent at least eighteen different railroad companies. Walkways are built up to some of the vehicles so that visitors can look inside a passenger car or the cab of a steam locomotive. Guides explain what it was like to work as a locomotive fireman or a Pullman sleeping-car porter.

Visitors entering from the Lobby see the original 1975 hall, with its gently curving, four-track display area, off to the right. Measuring 320 feet long by 150 feet wide, it is tall enough to house two buildings, Steinman Station and Stewart Junction Railway Education Center. Stairs lead down to a pit beneath track #2, where visitors can inspect the underside of a steam locomotive.

In 1995, the museum opened an extension to the original building that doubled the display space to nearly 100,000 square feet, bringing the total Rolling Stock Hall length to 640 feet. This newer section, which lies to the left on entering from the Lobby, was designed to replicate the open, airy feel of a nineteenth- or early-twentieth-century urban train shed. With a skylight roof and some glass walls, it has been dubbed Railroaders' Hall. At the east end is a permanent exhibit of plaques listing the names of men and women who work or have worked as railroad employees. An overhead catwalk gives visitors a panoramic view into both the original hall and the extension.

Alcoves and side aisles in the Rolling Stock Hall hold smaller displays that interpret other aspects of railroad life and technology. In the museum's collection are hundreds of items that illustrate the objects and culture of railroading, including signals, brakemen's lanterns, different kinds of rails, track-maintenance tools, dining-car equipment and china, Pullman sleeping-car items such as blankets and a porter's jacket, advertising posters, calendars, timetables, and employee passes.

3 STEINMAN STATION

It may be relatively easy for the museum to add locomotives and cars to its collection, but not so with railroad buildings, yet they, too, are an integral part of the industry's story. To help tell the story of railroading in rural Pennsylvania, a depot was constructed inside the Rolling Stock Hall.

In 1988, the museum opened Steinman Station, a full-size re-creation of a typical 1915 small-town depot. On entering the Rolling Stock Hall, visitors find themselves standing on the platform of the station, next to a passenger train that seems as if it is ready to depart. This combination passenger and freight station houses a stationmaster's office, waiting room, ticket office, and baggage room. Here, visitors can also watch historical railroad films from the museum's collection and an interpretive orientation video.

JOSEPH LUPPINO

STATION 3

RAILROADS IN POPULAR CULTURE

DAVID DUNN

4 STEWART JUNCTION RAILWAY EDUCATION CENTER

The forty-five-hundred-square-foot Stewart Junction Railway Education Center, which opened in September 2000, is housed in a two-story building with a Victorian freight-station facade in the northwest corner of the Rolling Stock Hall. Funded by the North American Railway Foundation, the $700,000 facility is named for the late James H. Stewart Jr., of Harrisburg, who headed that organization.

Nine distinct operating train layouts with models donated by several manufacturers and private donors are set in an exhibit, replete with railroad ephemera. The center provides an effective venue for educational programs for families, schools, and scouts. Hands-on displays and activities give both children and adults a sense of participation. Numerous model-train layouts are targeted to different age ranges—from preschool to adult. The centerpiece is a 115-foot-long G scale layout, with 318 feet of track winding through seven towns. Aimed at ages eight through adult, it's designed to give visitors a chance to operate a real railroad in miniature, not just run a model train around a circle of track. Kids or adults are assigned different jobs, learning how to cooperate and communicate to complete a complex task, just as occurs daily on a real railroad. Other dioramas have different themes, and trains, representing the "fallen flags" of Pennsylvania's railroads, roll along above visitors' heads on tracks suspended from the ceiling.

5 ART GALLERY

Opened in 2001, the Art Gallery occupies a space on the second floor of the museum, near the Research Center, and is used for changing exhibits. It is reached by taking an elevator or stairs from the Lobby, or by climbing a stairway in the Rolling Stock Hall and crossing the overhead walkway. The museum owns or has on long-term loan many original pieces of art, illustration, and portraiture. Among its holdings are lifesize oil paintings of Pennsylvania Railroad presidents, including a c. 1903 John Singer Sargent portrait of Alexander Cassatt, brother of painter Mary Cassatt and president of the PRR from 1899 to 1906. Other art-

DAVID DUNN

work includes several oil paintings by Grif Teller, which he created for the Pennsylvania Railroad calendar series (1925–58), and advertising illustrations. Among the best-known Teller paintings in the museum's collection is the signature piece *On Time!*, which appeared on the railroad's 1932 calendar.

6 RESTORATION SHOP

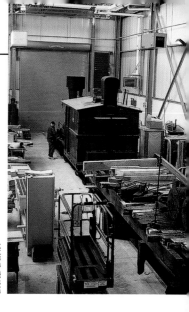

Behind the Rolling Stock Hall, and not normally open to visitors, is the fifty-four-hundred-square-foot Restoration Shop, opened in 1999. The facility was built to provide a permanent location in which restorers can work, rather than carry their tools to various work sites, and to create an all-season indoor space so that work can continue regardless of weather conditions. A sixty-foot-long pit beneath the rails allows workers to get underneath locomotives and cars and stand upright to make inspections or work on restoration.

Inside the building are a machine shop, wood shop, electrical shop, welding area, and paint spray booth. The machine shop is equipped with a lathe, milling machine, shear, and plate bender. Woodworking tools include a band saw, radial-arm saw, joiner, shaper, table saw, and planer—high-quality machinery capable of turning out cabinet-grade work. Working in the shop are a handful of full-time and temporary museum staff, and a pool of some twenty restoration volunteers, perhaps five of whom are working on any given day or weekend.

Based on intensive research, restoration is carried out with respect for the integrity of the original construction. Contemporary substitutions of materials or structural members are internally marked as such. To the degree possible, workers try to learn how an object was crafted before attempting to repair or restore it. In cases where too much of an original material is gone, workers re-create parts and fittings, using the original pieces as patterns.

DAVID DUNN

7 RESTORATION YARD

STEVE PANOPOULOS

The five-and-one-half-acre Restoration Yard on the west end of the property is what most people see first as they approach the museum from the center of Strasburg. Locomotives and cars stored here reflect varying degrees of restoration. Because fewer of these pieces are restored than those that are kept indoors, most are not open for visitors to go inside except by special arrangement. The yard is open frequently but not always; access depends on weather and scheduling. When it is open, guided tours are frequently available. An operating 1928 Reading Company one-hundred-foot-long turntable—which is an exhibit in itself and the largest artifact in the museum collection—is used to move engines and cars from one radial display track to another as pieces arrive or leave the property, enter or leave the Rolling Stock Hall, or move to or from the restoration shop.

8 ROBERT A. SPROUT MEMORIAL RESEARCH CENTER

Named for the second president of the Friends of the Railroad Museum, the Research Center consists of a library and archives containing a vast written, photographic, and audio record of the railroad industry from the 1830s to the present. Among its holdings are records, minutes, maps, drawings, manuscripts, and other corporate documents covering twelve hundred North American railroads. Also in the collection are color transparencies, photographic prints, and negative and glass-plate images, including official photographs and negatives from several companies in the railroad industry; promotional and safety films, videotapes, and audiotaped oral histories; books, atlases, technical manuals, company and union magazines, trade journals, and operating rulebooks; and other railroad-related artifacts, such as advertising ephemera, annual reports, dining-car menus, postcards, and tickets.

The museum's library and archives is one of the largest railroad-only research facilities in the country and is used by more than five hundred researchers each year. Appointments to use the research center must be made in advance (see page 47).

LOCOMOTIVE AND ROLLING STOCK COLLECTION

The heart of the museum collection is its assortment of more than one hundred locomotives and cars. These include steam, diesel, and electric locomotives; passenger and freight cars; cabooses; and maintenance and training cars. Some have been donated, some have been purchased, and some have been loaned from other museums. They have come from many sources over several decades of time. Vehicles are grouped below by type and function. Builders' construction numbers are indicated by the abbreviation C/N, and museum accession numbers are listed in parentheses at the end of the entries. Items loaned to the museum are so indicated, as are items in the collection that are housed, operated, or displayed off-site.

STEAM SWITCHING LOCOMOTIVES

The need to shuffle cars and rearrange them in railroad yards was met by small but powerful switching locomotives. Most of them have short wheelbases, with few or no leading or trailing wheels, only powered driving wheels, because of their need to get around the sharp curves of industrial siding tracks. Tank engines (designated with a T) have no tenders but instead carry their water supply in a tank or tanks slung over or astride the boiler, and their fuel in a bin behind the cab. Fireless engines, used around industrial plants where an open flame would be a hazard or where a source of abundant steam is present, such as at a steam-driven power plant, use a cylindrical pressure vessel in place of a traditional boiler. They are recharged periodically from a stationary steam source; they are tank locomotives in that they hold a supply of steam and need no tender to carry fuel or water, but they are not designated with a letter T.

- No. 3, Olomana: 0-4-2T type, Waimanolo Sugar Co., Waimanolo, Hawaii, narrow-gauge sugar plantation locomotive, built May 1883 by Baldwin Locomotive Works, Philadelphia. C/N 6753. On loan from Smithsonian Institution.
- No. 13: 0-6-0T type, Brooklyn Eastern District Terminal Railroad, Class C, built 1919 by H. K. Porter Locomotive Works, Pittsburgh. Built for U.S. Navy; sold to BEDT and operated into the

early 1960s in dock service, switching freight cars onto and off car floats (barges that transferred railcars across New York Harbor); later owned by an excursion carrier, Rail Tours, Inc. C/N 6369 (RR77.1.1A).
- No. 94: 0-4-0 type, Pennsylvania Railroad Class A5s, built January 1917 by PRR Juniata Shops, Altoona, Pa. C/N 3191 (RR79.40.3A).
- No. 111: 0-4-0 fireless type, Bethlehem Steel Co., built Feb-

ruary 1941 by Heisler Locomotive Works, Erie, Pa. C/N 58 (RR72.7).
- No. 1187: 0-4-0 Camelback type (cab is mounted astride the boiler to accommodate wide firebox designed to burn anthracite coal), Philadelphia & Reading Railway Class A-4b, built March 1903 by Burnham, Williams & Co. (Baldwin Locomotive Works). Built for P&R, later sold for industrial use at Birdsboro, Pa.; sold in 1962 to Strasburg Rail

Road, where it was renumbered as No. 4. C/N 21831. One of only three surviving camelback locomotives in America. On loan from Strasburg Rail Road Co.

- No. 1251: 0-6-0T type, Philadelphia & Reading Railway Class B4a, built September 1918 by P&R Reading Shops, Reading, Pa. Used into the 1960s as a shop switcher at the Reading Locomotive Shops. Later used in excursion service by Rail Tours, Inc. C/N 2306 (RR 72.18.1A).
- No. 1670: 0-6-0 type, Pennsylvania Railroad Class B6sb, built March 1916 by PRR Juniata Shops, Altoona, Pa. C/N 3042 (RR 79.40.7A).
- No. 4094: 0-8-0 fireless type, Pennsylvania Power and Light Co. Class 8-30, built January

No. 1251. STEVE PANOPOULOS

1940 by Heisler Locomotive Works, Erie, Pa. The largest fireless engine ever built. It is streamlined, a design treatment usually reserved for passenger locomotives. Exhibited at the

1940 New York World's Fair. Built as No. 4 for Hammermill Paper Co. at Erie, Pa., resold to PP&L in 1941, renumbered 4094 and assigned to Hauto, Pa. C/N 47 (RR 72.20.1A).

STEAM FREIGHT LOCOMOTIVES

Freight locomotives are characterized by relatively smaller driving wheels that produce more power than speed. In most cases, they have two leading wheels—one on each side—to guide them through curves and switches at moderate main-line speeds.

- No. 20, Tahoe: 2-6-0 type, Virginia & Truckee Railroad, built January 1875 by Baldwin Locomotive Works, Philadelphia. Baldwin Class 8-28d. A classic example of nineteenth-century locomotive engineering and design. C/N 3687 (RR 72.34.1A).
- No. 520: 2-8-2 type, Pennsylvania Railroad Class L1s, built December 1916 by Baldwin Locomotive Works, Philadelphia. One of 574 of this type built. C/N 44565 (RR 79.40.5A).
- No. 757: 2-8-4 type, New York, Chicago & St. Louis Railroad (Nickel Plate Road) Class S-2, built August 1944 by Lima Locomotive Works, Lima, Ohio. Dual service engine; designed for fast freight service (Chicago–Erie– Buffalo) but capable of operating in passenger service as well. C/N 8665 (RR 72.22.1A).
- No. 1187: 2-8-0 type, Pennsylvania Railroad Class H3, built January 1888 by PRR Altoona Shops, Altoona, Pa. Sold to John P. Dyer Quarry, Monocacy, Pa. Reacquired by PRR in 1939 and restored for historical display at

No. 6755.

New York World's Fair. C/N 1235 (RR 79.40.6A).
- No. 2846: 2-8-0 type, Pennsylvania Railroad Class H6sb, built November 1905 by Burnham, Williams & Co. (Baldwin Locomotive Works), Philadelphia. C/N 26744 (RR 79.40.9).
- No. 6755: 4-8-2 type, Pennsylvania Railroad Class M1b, built June 1930 by PRR Juniata Shops. Dual service engine; designed for fast freight service but capable of operating in pas-

senger service as well. Largest Pennsy steam locomotive to be preserved. C/N 4225 (RR 79.40.12A).
- No. 7688: 2-8-0 type, Pennsylvania Railroad Class H10s, built September 1915 by Lima Locomotive Works, Lima, Ohio. Only surviving Lima-built PRR locomotive. C/N 5063 (RR 79.40.14A).

STEAM PASSENGER LOCOMOTIVES

Passenger steam locomotives tend to have larger driving wheels that produce more speed than power. They also are usually equipped with four-wheel leading trucks to guide them through switches and curves at higher speed.

- No. 460: 4-4-2 type, Pennsylvania Railroad Class E6s, built September 1914 by PRR Juniata Shops, Altoona, Pa. "The Lindbergh Special" locomotive. C/N 2860 (RR 79.40.4A).
- No. 1223: 4-4-0 type, Pennsylvania Railroad Class D16sb, built November 1905 by PRR Juniata Shops, Altoona, Pa. C/N 1399 (RR 79.40.16A).
- No. 3750: 4-6-2 type, Pennsylvania Railroad Class K4s, built March 1920 by PRR Juniata Shops, Altoona, Pa. The most widely known steam passenger locomotive type on the Pennsylvania Railroad—425 of them were built from 1914 to 1928, and this is one of only two surviving members of the class. Pulled President Warren G. Harding's funeral train in 1923. C/N 3703 (RR79.40.8A).
- No. 5741: 4-6-0 type, Pennsylvania Railroad Class G5s, built November 1924 by PRR Juniata Shops. Used in Pittsburgh commuter service. C/N 3966 (RR 79.40.11).

No. 460. STEVE PANOPOULOS

- No. 7002: 4-4-2 type, Pennsylvania Railroad Class E7s, built August 1902 by PRR Juniata Shops, Altoona, Pa. Built as No. 8063 but renumbered 7002 by PRR publicity department about 1948 to represent a similar-looking PRR Class E2 locomotive of that number that PRR claimed in 1905 to have set an unverified steam locomotive speed world record of 127.1 mph. The original No. 7002 was scrapped in 1934. C/N 929 (RR 79.40.13A).

No. 1223 on display in Atlantic City, 1937.

STEAM LOGGING LOCOMOTIVES

Steep grades and sharp curves were the rule on temporary tracks that lumber companies hastily laid into stands of timber that were to be harvested before pulling up the rails and moving on to the next tract. This required locomotives with extreme power and flexibility rather than speed. As a result, several specialty designs evolved that used varying combinations of gearing rather than conventional rods and pins to transmit power to the wheels. The museum owns one of each of the three major types used in the state:

- No. 1: Three-truck Shay, Class 65-3, Ely-Thomas Lumber Co. (lettered to represent Leetonia Railway, a Pennsylvania lumber carrier), built December 1906 by Lima Locomotive and Machine Co., Lima, Ohio. Built as No. 4 for Enterprise Lumber Co., Simms, La., and resold several times before becoming Ely-Thomas Lumber Co. No. 2 working at Fenwick, W.Va. C/N 1799 (RR 72.24).
- No. 4: Class B Climax geared locomotive, W. H. Mason Lumber Co., built 1913 by Climax Manufacturing Co., Corry, Pa. Used at Ellamore, W.Va., by Moore, Keppel & Co., then by Middle Fork Railroad Co., then by W. H. Mason Lumber Co. at Elkins, W.Va. Sold to Edaville Corp. in

Logging Locomotive. This Leetonia Railway Shay No. 4 is a prototype of the museum's restored Shay No. 1.

1956 and displayed at Edaville Railroad, South Carver, Mass., until that railroad closed in the early 1990s. C/N 1237 (RR 92.15).

- No. 4: Two-truck Heisler, Class 53-8-38, built 1918 by Heisler Locomotive Works, Erie, Pa. C/N 1375 (RR 72.23).

FULL-SIZE REPRODUCTION STEAM LOCOMOTIVES

- John Stevens: Four-wheel type, reproduction of 1825 steam locomotive experiment, built 1939 by Pennsylvania Railroad Altoona Shops, Altoona, Pa. (RR 79.40.1).
- John Bull: 4-2-0 type, reproduction of 1831 Camden & Amboy Railroad locomotive No. 1. Original locomotive housed in Smithsonian Institution, Washington, D.C. Reproduction built May 1940 by Pennsylvania Railroad Altoona Works, Altoona, Pa., for 1940 New York World's Fair; operated in Railroads on Parade pageant. Operable condition. (RR 79.40.2A).

John Stevens Reproduction.

DIESEL-ELECTRIC SWITCHING LOCOMOTIVES

Most diesel-electric switching locomotives were built with the cab at one extreme end to improve visibility for the crew in the stop-and-start, coupling-and-uncoupling maneuvers that characterized their work.

- Unnumbered: B type (four powered wheels), 5-ton narrow-gauge locomotive, Model BFA, Lone Star Cement Co., Hudson, N.Y., built March 26, 1951, by Brookville Locomotive Works, Brookville, Pa. Built for 36-inch-gauge track, powered by a Ford flathead V8/239 motor. After retirement, used in children's play area at day-care center in Lansdale, Pa.,

before coming to museum. Light locomotive of the type used in logging, mining, plantation, or construction work. C/N 3744 (RR 97.32).
- No. 1: 18-ton switching locomotive, Pennsylvania Power & Light Co. Holtwood Dam, built 1949 by Plymouth Locomotive Works, Plymouth, Ohio. Operable condition. (For museum use; not accessioned.)

- No. 81: B-B type, Maryland & Pennsylvania Railroad, Model NW2, 1,000 horsepower, built 1946 by Electro-Motive Division of General Motors Corp., La Grange, Ill. Small railroads often used switchers for all kinds of service; this engine pulled the last Maryland & Pennsylvania ("Ma & Pa") passenger train out of Baltimore on August 31, 1954. C/N 4161 (RR 97.34).

- No. 701: B-B type, Monongahela Connecting Railroad, Model C-415, 1,500 horsepower, built July 1968 by Alco Products (formerly American Locomotive Co.), Schenectady, N.Y. Used around Pittsburgh-area steel mills owned by Jones & Laughlin Steel; railroad also was owned by J&L. The C-415 model used a slightly off-center cab design; this version has a lower cab roof that enabled it to operate in the restricted clearances of an industrial setting. Retired 1992. C/N 6005-1 (RR 92.8).

- No. 1200: B-B type, U.S. Navy, Model S-12, 1,200 horsepower, built 1951 by Baldwin Locomotive Works, Philadelphia. It was assigned as U.S. Navy No. 65-00369 at the Earle Weapons Station, Earle, N.J. C/N 75709 (RR 98.2).

DIESEL-ELECTRIC FREIGHT LOCOMOTIVES

The versatile road-switcher type diesel unit, designed for intercity freight service but capable of performing passenger service or switching operations, evolved as a practical step from the early streamlined-cab type units of the 1930s and 1940s.

- Unnumbered: A1A-A1A type, Alaska Railroad Model RS-1 road switcher, 1,000 horsepower, built 1941 by American Locomotive Co. for the Atlanta & St. Andrews Bay Railroad as No. 902. During World War II, requisitioned by the U.S. Army Transportation Corps and renumbered as No. 8011. From 1947 to 1951, this unit and thirty-four others were sent to Alaska for use on the U.S. government-owned Alaska Railroad as No. 1034. It returned to the U.S. Army in November 1956 as No. 8011. It was transferred to the U.S. Department of Transportation and renumbered as No. 013 in July 1975. The unit was donated to the Smithsonian Institution in September 1983 and has been on loan to the museum since then. C/N 69427.

No. 7006. RICHARD M. GLADULICH

- No. 2233: B-B type road switcher, Pennsylvania Railroad Class EF22 (EMD Model GP30), 2,250 horsepower, built April 1963 by the Electro-Motive Division of General Motors Corp., La Grange, Ill. An example of the first of the "second generation" of diesel locomotives on the Pennsylvania Railroad. C/N 28141. (RR 98.35).

- No. 7006: B-B type road switcher, Pennsylvania Railroad, Class ERS17 (EMD Model GP9), 1,750 horsepower, built 1955 by the Electro-Motive Division of General Motors Corp., La Grange, Ill. One of a fleet of 310 GP9 units whose arrival between 1955 and 1959 helped retire the last of PRR main-line steam. (RR 85.27).

DIESEL-ELECTRIC PASSENGER LOCOMOTIVE

Diesel-electric streamlined passenger locomotives first operated in Pennsylvania in regular scheduled service on the Baltimore & Ohio Railroad in the 1930s. After World War II, B&O expanded its fleet, and most of the other major intercity passenger carriers that served the state—PRR, New York Central, Lackawanna, Erie, and to a lesser extent, Reading and Nickel Plate Road—acquired fleets of them as well.

No. 5901. ALLAN MARTIN

- No. 5901: A1A-A1A type stream-lined cab-unit passenger engine, Pennsylvania Railroad Class EP20 (EMD Class E7), 2,000 horsepower, built September 1945 by the Electro-Motive Division of General Motors Corp., La Grange, Ill. One of the first two diesel road locomotives on the Pennsylvania Railroad; used initially on the Harrisburg–Detroit leg of the New York–Detroit Red Arrow passenger train. Later used also on the Broadway Limited, Spirit of St. Louis, and other feature passenger trains. PRR eventually owned a total of 134 units of the E7 and E8 types (introduced in 1950, the E8 was the 2,250-horsepower successor model to the E7). C/N 3357 (RR 76.37).

ELECTRIC SWITCHING LOCOMOTIVES

Relatively few North American railroads employed electrification, and of those that did, most employed electric locomotives mainly for road freight or road passenger service. As a result, electric switching units were rare.

- No. 3: Ore dock shunter, Pennsylvania Railroad narrow-gauge dock locomotive, built c. 1912 by Baldwin Locomotive Works, Philadelphia. Used at PRR Whiskey Island unloading facility on Lake Erie at Cleveland, Ohio. Powered by 250 volts collected from an energized third rail. (RR 2000.41).
- No. 5690: C type, Pennsylvania Railroad Class B1 switching unit, built December 1934 by PRR Altoona Works, Altoona, Pa. Rated at 570 horsepower. Used to switch passenger cars at major stations in PRR electrified territory, including at Philadelphia and Harrisburg. Powered by 11,000 volts AC collected from an energized overhead wire. C/N 4263. (RR 73.9).

No. 5690. RICHARD M. GLADULICH

ELECTRIC FREIGHT LOCOMOTIVE

A few North American railroads used electric locomotives for freight service. Only a handful continue to do so, mostly for captive coal-mine-to-power-plant use, and none in Pennsylvania.

- No. 4465: C-C type, Pennsylvania Railroad Class E44 main-line freight unit. Built July 1963 by General Electric, Erie, Pa. Rated at 4,400 horsepower. Later became Penn Central No. 4465 and then Amtrak No. 502. Final unit constructed of 66-member class of PRR E44 electric locomotives built from 1960 to 1963. Powered by 11,000 volts AC collected from overhead wire. C/N 33411. (RR 91.6).

ELECTRIC PASSENGER LOCOMOTIVES

It is in passenger service, with the ability to move large numbers of people in densely packed population centers, that electric locomotives most dramatically show off their potential. The proof of this is that Amtrak continues to use electric propulsion for its Boston–New York–Philadelphia–Baltimore–Washington service on the Northeast Corridor route.

- Nos. 3936–3937: 2-B+B-2 type, Pennsylvania Railroad Class DD-1 passenger unit, built May 1911 by PRR Juniata Shops. Later renumbered 4780–4781. Initially built to enable PRR to move passenger trains through its Hudson River Tunnels into the massive 1910 Pennsylvania Station complex in Manhattan. Also later used for switching service. Rated at 3,150 horsepower. Powered by 650 volts DC; obtains current from shoe sliding on energized third rail beside track. C/Ns 2244-2 for 3936 and 2244-1 for 3937. (RR 79.40.10).
- No. 4800: 2-C+C-2 type, Pennsylvania Railroad Class GG1, built August 1934 by Baldwin Locomotive Works, Eddystone, Pa., and General Electric, Erie, Pa. Prototype of the highly successful 139-member GG1 class of passenger locomotives; also later used for freight service. Rated at 4,620 horsepower. Powered by 11,000 volts AC collected from overhead wire. Donated by Lancaster Chapter, National Railway Historical Society. C/N 11646. (RR 2000.20).

No. 4800. STEVE PANOPOULOS

- No. 4859: 2-C+C-2 type, Pennsylvania Railroad Class GG1, built December 1937 by PRR Altoona Works, Altoona, Pa. Rated at 4,620 horsepower. Pulled the first Philadelphia–Harrisburg electric train on January 15, 1938. Later used for both passenger and freight service; hauled the last GG1-powered freight train for Conrail in November 1979, Enola, Pa., to Edge Moor, Del. Displayed at Harrisburg, Pa., Amtrak station. Powered by 11,000 volts AC

collected from overhead wire. C/N 4326. (x86.52).
- No. 4935: 2-C+C-2 type, Pennsylvania Railroad Class GG1, built March 1943 by PRR Juniata Shops, Altoona, Pa. Rated at 4,620 horsepower. Powered by 11,000 volts AC collected from overhead wire. Later owned by Penn Central and then Amtrak; was restored to PRR appearance in 1977 and operated from then until its retirement in that livery. C/N 4434. (RR 83.30).

DIESEL- AND GAS-POWERED SELF-PROPELLED PASSENGER COACHES

Self-propelled coaches offered a perfect solution for branch-line and some commuter-route use, where enough business existed to justify train service, but not enough to support the higher cost of running a locomotive-hauled train.

- No. 21: Mack-J. G. Brill Model AC Railbus, built November 1921. Former Lewistown, Milton, and Watsontown Railway No. 20, ex-Pennsylvania Railroad. (RR 2002.2)
- No. 40: RDC-1 type, Lehigh Valley Railroad, Rail Diesel Car, built August 1951 by Budd Co., Philadelphia. Used on Hazleton–Lehighton, Pa., shuttle to connect with LV main-line Buffalo–New York passenger trains. Sold December 1962 to Reading Co. and renumbered as No. 9163. C/N 5410. (RR 84.36).
- No. 9167: RDC-1 type, Reading Co. Rail Diesel Car, built March 1953 by Budd Co., Philadelphia. Built as New Haven Railroad No. 40, later became Penn Central No. 40, then Reading/Southeastern Pennsylvania Transportation Authority No. 9167. Operable

No. 40.

condition. On loan to Bellefonte Railroad Historical Society, Bellefonte, Pa. C/N 5718 (x84.14).

ELECTRIC-POWERED MULTIPLE-UNIT PASSENGER CARS

After conducting experiments elsewhere, the Pennsylvania Railroad began electrified commuter service between Philadelphia and Paoli, Pa., in 1914, and later expanded the network to most of its Philadelphia-area suburban routes. Starting in 1931, the Reading Co. also electrified most of its Philadelphia commuter routes. Both used the technology of electrically propelled motorized coaches that could be coupled together and operated from one control position, hence the "multiple-unit," or MU, designation. Later the concept was expanded to high-speed intercity equipment as well.

- Nos. 246 and 247: Pioneer III series multiple-unit stainless-steel commuter coaches, Pennsylvania Railroad, built 1958 by Budd Co., Philadelphia. Subsequently owned by Penn Central and finally Southeastern Pennsylvania Transportation Authority. Powered by 11,000 volts AC collected from overhead wire. The first lightweight stainless-steel electric commuter cars in America, they were the forerunners of several generations of Silverliner electric MU cars that are still running in Philadelphia commuter service for SEPTA. (RR 99.9).

No. 800.

- No. 607: Multiple-unit steel commuter coach, Pennsylvania Railroad Class MP-54-El, built 1913 by Pressed Steel Car Co., McKees Rocks, Pa. Powered by 11,000 volts AC collected from overhead wire. One of a fleet of cars used in Philadelphia-area commuter service to Paoli, Chestnut Hill, Manayunk, and West Chester, Pa.; Trenton, N.J.; and Wilmington, Del. Also used in local service between New York and Trenton, N.J.; Philadelphia and Harrisburg; and Chester, Pa., Baltimore; and Washington. Later owned by Penn Central. (RR 76.36).

- No. 800: Multiple-unit steel commuter coach, Reading Co. Class EPA, built 1931 by Harlan & Hollingsworth plant of Bethlehem Steel Corp., Wilmington, Del. Powered by 11,000 volts AC collected from overhead wire. First Reading electric multiple-unit coach, used in Philadelphia commuter service to suburban Chestnut Hill, Hatboro, West Trenton, Norristown, and Doylestown, Pa. (RR 80.48).

- No. 860: Multiple-unit high-speed intercity stainless-steel Metroliner passenger car, built January 1968 by Budd Co., Philadelphia, for Pennsylvania Railroad, but ownership changed with PRR's merger into Penn Central on February 1, 1968. Metroliner cars did not enter revenue service until 1969. Later owned by Amtrak. Configured as a 60-seat coach/snack-bar car. Powered by 11,000 volts AC collected from overhead wire. Part of the 61-member Metroliner fleet that was designed to introduce 160 mph service (actual speeds were 110–120 mph) to the Northeast Corridor between New York, Philadelphia, Baltimore, and Washington. (RR 96.6).

FREIGHT CARS

The backbone of North American railroading is its fleet of freight cars, each purpose-built to handle specific kinds of loads. Boxcars carry lumber, merchandise, or grain; hopper cars carry stone, ore, or coal; covered hoppers carry grain, dry chemicals, plastic pellets, cement, sand, or ballast; gondolas carry steel, lumber, stone, or scrap; tank cars carry liquids such as chemicals, soap, gasoline, or corn syrup; refrigerator cars carry perishables such as dressed meat, produce, frozen food, or fresh flowers; and flatcars carry machinery, farm equipment, military equipment (including tanks), merchandise, or lumber.

- No. DLA90614: Steel boxcar, U.S. Air Force, Chambersburg Supply Depot (Letterkenny Army Depot), Chambersburg, Pa., built April 1953 by Pullman-Standard. Originally numbered USAFX 26694.

- (For museum use; not accessioned.)
- No. DLA90613: Steel boxcar, U.S. Army, Chambersburg Supply Depot (Letterkenny Army Depot), Chambersburg, Pa., built May 1951 by Pullman-Standard.

- Originally numbered USAX 26152. (For museum use; not accessioned.)
- No. 1818: Wooden hopper car, Pittsburgh, Youngstown & Ashtabula Railroad, Class GG, built July 1895 by Barney &

Smith Car Co. of Dayton, Oh. Oldest PRR freight car in existence. (RR 79.40.20).

- No. 4556: Steel three-dome tank car, built c.1920s by American Car & Foundry Co., specific plant where built is unknown. Capacity 4,551 gallons. (RR 97.36).
- No. 5078: Composite (wood and steel) boxcar, Reading Railroad, U.S. Railroad Administration design, 30' length, Class 1001-B, built 1918, builder unknown. (RR 77.96).
- No. 8148: Wooden gondola, Delaware & Hudson Railroad, built December 1906 by American Car & Foundry, Berwick, Pa. (RR 74.7.2).
- No. 14518: Steel offset-side twin hopper car, Lehigh & New England Railroad, built c. 1920, later owned by Pennsylvania Power & Light Co. Builder unknown, original number of this car unknown, number applied in random selection from original number series. (RR 72.43).
- No. 19607: Wooden boxcar, Delaware & Hudson Railroad, 30' length, built April 1907 by American Car & Foundry Co., Berwick, Pa. (RR 74.7.1).
- No. 32367: Steel covered-hopper car, Pennsylvania Railroad Class H34A, built June 1955 by PRR Altoona Car Shops, Altoona, Pa. Former Penn Central No. 32367. (RR 2001.62).
- No. 33164: Steel hopper car, Pennsylvania Railroad, Class GL, built October 1898 by Pressed Steel Car Co., Pittsburgh. (RR 79.40.26).
- No. 38358: Steel flatcar, U.S. Army, built June 1953 by Magor Car Co., Clifton, N.J. Later transferred to Department of Defense, Navy Inventory Control Point, Mechanicsburg, Pa. (For museum use; not accessioned.)

No. 255750.

- No. 38482: Steel boxcar, Pennsylvania Railroad, Class X29, 40' length, built January 1930 by Standard Steel Car Co. Reassigned to work equipment service as PRR No. 490270 in July 1961. Formerly Penn Central 38482, original PRR No. 55351. (RR 99.67).
- No. 39502: Steel flatcar, U.S. Army, built June 1953 by Magor Car Co., Clifton, N.J. Later transferred to Department of Defense, Navy Inventory Control Point, Mechanicsburg, Pa. (For museum use; not accessioned.)
- No. 57708: Wooden refrigerator car with steel underframe, Fruit Growers Express, built 1924, builder unknown. (RR 92.6).
- No. 75073: Wooden boxcar with steel underframe, Lehigh Valley Railroad, 40' length, built June 1930, builder unknown. (RR 72.44).
- No. 78847: Steel hopper car, Reading Company, Class HTh, built c. 1920s by Reading Shops, St. Clair, Pa. (RR 72.45).
- No. 255750: Steel covered-hopper car, Pennsylvania Railroad Class H30A, built August 1951, by PRR Altoona Shops, Altoona, Pa. Acquired from Metro-North Commuter Railroad as its MNCX No. 021. (RR 88.3).
- No. 473567: Steel flatcar with wooden deck, Pennsylvania Rail-

road, Class FM, built November 1909 by American Car & Foundry Co. Car originally owned by subsidiary Pittsburgh, Cincinnati, Chicago, & St. Louis Railroad No. 939691. Converted to a container car at Mahoningtown in July 1931 as No. 473567. Converted back to a flatcar in 1951. Later used to transport John Bull replica steam locomotive. (RR 79.40.27).

- No. 500487: Steel ore jenny, Pennsylvania Railroad, built 1964 by Samuel Rea Shops, Hollidaysburg, Pa. Originally PRR No. 13182. Used to transport Venezulean iron ore between Philadelphia and Pittsburgh. Renumbered as Conrail No. 500487 in the 1970s. (RR 99.43.1).
- No. 800264, Steel Gondola, Pennsylvania Railroad, class GS, 40' length, built May 1902 by Pressed Steel Car Co. Originally built as Toledo, Walhonding Valley and Ohio No. 2284. (RR 2001.61).
- No. 500001: Steel tank car, Pennsylvania Railroad, Class TP-1, built January 1966 by PRR Samuel Rea Shops, Hollidaysburg, Pa. Capacity 38,000 gallons; nicknamed "Rail Whale." Later owned by Penn Central, then Conrail; renumbered as Conrail No. 70899. (RR 98.34).

PASSENGER CARS

People ride passenger cars to and from work, for business travel, or for leisure. Trips can range from a few miles to a cross-country journey taking several days. Cars used in passenger-train service include baggage and mail cars, day coaches, dining cars, lounge cars, parlor cars, overnight sleepers with seats that convert to beds, observation cars, and, for the use of railroad executives on official business, office cars, also known as business cars. Early travel was rough, dusty, and often unreliable. The average passenger ate out of a paper bag and slept overnight in a coach seat. Luxury travel in Pullmans or first-class was limited to upper-income passengers.

- No. B: Wooden combination passenger-baggage car, Cumberland Valley Railroad, built 1855 by CVRR shops, Chambersburg, Pa. Equipped with link-and-pin couplers. (RR 79.40.15).
- Lotos Club: Steel eight-section restaurant-sleeper with solarium-lounge end, built October 1913 by Pullman Co. as ten-section observation-lounge car El Quivira for California Limited, rebuilt and renamed in September 1936, Plan No. 4025D. Used on many railroads, including Baltimore & Ohio and Pittsburgh & Lake Erie. (RR 81.1).
- Scioto Rapids: Steel streamlined sleeper with ten compartments and six double bedrooms, Pennsylvania Railroad, built 1949 by Budd Co., Philadelphia. Operated in a pool for main-line New York–Midwest overnight PRR trains. Later owned by Penn Central and then Amtrak. (RR 97.18).
- Tower View: Steel streamlined observation-sleeper, Pennsylvania Railroad, Class POS21, built 1948 by Pullman Co., Plan No. 4133. Usually assigned to PRR's premier New York–Chicago train, Broadway Limited. Assigned road No. 8420 for internal accounting purposes but never lettered with that identification. (RR 72.31).
- No. 1: Stainless-steel streamlined observation-coach car, Reading Co., built 1937 by Budd Co., Philadelphia. Served as one of two observation-coach cars on Reading's Philadelphia–Jersey City, N.J., Crusader, the first stainless-steel streamlined train in the East. Sold to Canadian National Railways, and later became VIA Rail Canada No. 304. (RR 86.24).
- No. 6: Wooden baggage car, Pennsylvania Railroad Class Ba, built 1882, builder unknown. (RR 79.40.17).
- No. 35: Wooden combination baggage-passenger car, Buffalo & Susquehanna Railroad, later part of Baltimore & Ohio Railroad, and then Wellsville, Addison & Galeton Railroad, built 1906 as a buffet-passenger coach by Barney & Smith Car Co., Dayton, Ohio. (RR 97.38).
- No. 81: Steel Railway Post Office car, Baltimore & Ohio Railroad, built c. 1920s, builder unknown.

No. 3556.

Interior of No. 8177.

Retired from the Cincinnati and St. Louis Railway Post Office (RPO) service on April 5, 1968. (RR 72.39).
- No. 203: Steel business car, Western Maryland Railway, built 1914 by Pullman Co., Plan No. 2793. Used for officials traveling, inspecting track, or conducting meetings. Exterior of car is steel made to resemble wood siding (RR 72.50).
- No. 835: Steel coach, Western Maryland Railway, built 1917 by Pullman Co. In later years, used as a rider car to Western Maryland business car No. 203. (RR 97.33).
- No. 1006: Steel coach, Pennsylvania Railroad Class P70, built c. 1916–22, builder unknown. Designed and first built in 1907, the P70 class was the first mass-produced steel day-coach design in America. It was developed because of the need for fire

safety and structural integrity in operating a high volume of trains through PRR's tunnels under the Hudson River in and out of Pennsylvania Station, which was opened in 1910 in Manhattan. (RR 73.17).
- No. 1189: Steel dining car, Reading Co., Class DPA, rebuilt from former Class DCE car, c. 1916. (RR 72.38).
- No. 1552: Steel parlor-lounge car, Lehigh Valley Railroad, built 1927 by Pullman Co. Formerly named White Diamond, it was assigned to run between New York City, Allentown, Bethlehem, Wilkes-Barre, and Buffalo, N.Y., on LV train Black Diamond. (RR 72.64).
- No. 1650: Steel coach, Pennsylvania Railroad, Class P53, built March 1908 by PRR's Altoona Shops, Altoona, Pa. (RR 79.40.19).

- No. 1651: Steel coach, Pennsylvania Railroad, Class P58, built June 1906 by PRR Altoona Shops, Altoona, Pa. Generally regarded to be the first all-steel passenger coach on the PRR, it was an experimental hybrid design that used many wooden components. Developed in response to telescoping accidents caused by wooden passenger cars. (RR 79.40.18).
- No. 3556: Wooden coach, Pennsylvania Railroad, Class Pf, built August 1886 by PRR Altoona Shops, Altoona, Pa. (RR 79.40.21).
- No. 4639: Wooden combination baggage-passenger car, Pennsylvania Railroad, Class Og, built March 1895 by PRR Altoona Shops, Altoona, Pa. (RR 79.40.22).
- No. 5403: Wooden baggage-mail car, Pennsylvania Railroad, Class Bc, built 1892 by PRR Altoona Shops, Altoona, Pa. (RR 79.40.23).
- No. 6076: Wooden Adams Express baggage car, Pennsylvania Railroad, Class Bd, built 1899 by PRR Altoona Shops, Altoona, Pa. (RR 79.40.24).
- No. 8177: Wooden coach, Pennsylvania Railroad, passenger coach, Class Ph, built 1896 by PRR Altoona Shops, Altoona, Pa. (RR 79.40.25).
- No. 9356: Steel baggage car, Pennsylvania Railroad, Class B60B, built 1928 by St. Louis Car Co., St. Louis, Mo. Entered service as an express-messenger baggage car. Originally numbered 8863; renumbered 9356 in 1946. (RR 85.37).

CABOOSES

Traveling at the rear of a freight train, the caboose functions as a rolling office in which the conductor manages paperwork and serves as the place from which the crew keeps an eye on the train ahead, from a cupola or a bay window. Crews were often assigned to specific cabooses and lived in them, sleeping on bunks and cooking on a coal stove while laying over at an outlying point awaiting their assignment to move a freight train back to their home terminal. With improved telecommunications and telemetry and smaller crews today, most railroads have eliminated cabooses except in special local circumstances.

- No. 67: Steel caboose, Monongahela Railway, built 1949, builder unknown. On loan from Smithsonian Institution.
- No. 508: Steel bay-window caboose, Pittsburgh & Lake Erie Railroad, built 1950 by P&LE shops, McKee's Rocks, Pa. (RR 92.11).
- No. 2606: Four-wheel wooden caboose, Lehigh Valley Railroad, built c. 1910, builder unknown. Later owned by Williamsport & North Branch Railroad and also by C.W. Sones Lumber Co., Lycoming County. During restoration, underframe and wheels came from Lehigh & New England Railroad tunnel car No. 671, built 1908 and used on Lansford, Pa., side of Hauto Tunnel. (RR 97.39).
- No. 477947: Steel caboose, Pennsylvania Railroad, Class N5c, built July 1942 by PRR Altoona Car Shops, Altoona, Pa. Streamlined cupola design with porthole side windows. Later owned by Penn Central and then Conrail. Number displayed on car is not original number. Originally PRR No. 478007; later became Penn Central No. 23329 and Conrail No. 23175. (RR 90.4).
- No. 478396: Four-wheel wooden

No. 2606.

caboose, Pennsylvania Railroad, Class ND, built June 1913 by PRR Altoona Car Shops, Altoona, Pa. Originally owned by PRR subsidiary Northern Central Railway as PRR No. 488333; renumbered PRR No. 478396 in May 1920. Used on PRR Middle Division. Sold 1940 to Huntingdon & Broad Top Mountain Railroad and renumbered No. 16; transferred 1953 to H&BTM successor Everett Railroad, Everett, Pa.; transferred 1966 to Larry H. Williams, Saxton, Pa. (RR 98.55).

- No. 492015: Four-wheel wooden caboose, Pennsylvania Railroad, Class ND, built June 1906 by Wall Shops, Wall, Pa. Originally PRR No. 486362; renumbered PRR No. 476261 in May 1920; and made work equipment PRR 492015 in May 1934. Used on PRR Lines East until c.1960s. (Not accessioned; used as a parts source for the restoration of PRR No. 478396.)

NON-REVENUE AND MISCELLANEOUS CARS

Maintaining a railroad line in good condition requires vehicles that allow crews to inspect or repair the facilities, clean up debris after a wreck, and in winter, clear the track of snow and ice.

- Unnumbered: Motorized four-wheel, one-cylinder Fairmount section car. Former New York, Ontario, & Western Railway Class M2C (RR 77.90).
- Unnumbered: Wooden snow-plow, Coudersport & Port Allegany Railroad, Size 2, built c. 1895 by Russell Snowplow Co., Ridgway, Pa. (RR 80.50).
- Unnumbered: Four-wheel hand-powered track car, built c. 1890s for Philadelphia & Reading Railway, builder unknown. (RR 93.2).
- Unnumbered: Three-wheeled track velocipede, built c. 1880s by George S. Sheffield & Co., Three Rivers, Mich. (RR 80.32).
- M20: Motorized track car, formerly Reading Co. and Chesapeake & Ohio, built February 1956 by Fairmont Railway Motors, Inc., Fairmont, Minn. Class M-19. Commonly called a "speeder." Operable condition. (RR 91.7).
- No. 122: Motorized track car, formerly Central Railroad of New Jersey and Lehigh & New England Railroad, built 1944 by Fairmont Railway Motors, Inc., Fairmont, Minn. Model A3 (Series C). Commonly called a "speeder." (RR 75.2).
- No. 31188: Steel idler car, Conrail, built c. 1923. Used in conjunction with wreck derrick, formerly PRR Class F30 flatcar No. 470189. (RR 98.4).
- No. 45210: Steel 250-ton diesel-powered wreck derrick, Conrail, built December 1954 by Industrial Brownhoist, Bay City, Mich. formerly Erie Railroad No. 3302. The internal plant consists of two Cummins diesel engines, rated at 190 horsepower each, with twin Marine torque converters. Derrick was assigned to the Conrail wreck train based at Meadville (Pa.) Car Shop until 1978, and thereafter at Conway (Pa.) Yard until 1995. (RR 98.4).
- No. 490014: Horse Express car, Pennsylvania Railroad, Class B74B, formerly racehorse car Saratoga Springs, built August 1928 by PRR Altoona Car Shops, Altoona, Pa. Removed from revenue service March 1963 and renumbered 490014 for maintenance-of-way use in February 1964. Capacity 65,000 pounds, or twenty-four live horses. (For museum use; not accessioned.)
- No. 490398: Test weight car, Pennsylvania Railroad, Class YA, built June 1891 by PRR Altoona Shops, Altoona, Pa. Originally PRR No. 91068; renumbered PRR 191068; and then PRR 490398 in June 1905. Later became Conrail No. 80000. Used to calibrate weighing car scales. (RR 89.1.1).
- No. 492445: Steel air-brake instruction car, Pennsylvania Railroad, built March 1910 by Altoona Car Shops as a Class M70 railway post office car No. 6517. Converted to classroom use in June 1928 by Pitcairn Car Shops as air-brake instruction car and renumbered 492445. Car assigned to PRR Central Region. Training car for employees. (RR 77.99).

TROLLEY CAR

Street railways and trolley cars tended to run within cities or connect cities with nearby towns. Many started in the nineteenth century as horse-car lines and upgraded to electric power in the 1890–1900 period. Scranton, a pioneer city in electric railway development, operated the first commercial streetcar in 1886.

- No. 236: Steel Birney-type trolley car, Conestoga Traction Co., built 1926 by J.G. Brill Co., Philadelphia. Operable condition. On loan to Manheim Historical Society, Manheim, Pa. (RR 87.14).

For information on hours, research, programs, and activities at Railroad Museum of Pennsylvania, visit **www.rrmuseumpa.org** or call **717-687-8628**.

Further Reading

Anderson, Elaine. *The Central Railroad of New Jersey's First 100 Years: A Historical Survey.* Easton, Pa.: Center for Canal History and Technology, 1984.

Archer, Robert F. *A History of the Lehigh Valley Railroad, "The Route of the Black Diamond."* Berkeley, Calif.: Howell-North Books, 1977.

Baumgartner, Mahlon J., and Floyd G. Hoenstine. *The Allegheny Old Portage Railroad, 1834–1854.* Ebensburg, Pa.: Self-published, 1952.

Beaver, Roy C. *Bessemer & Lake Erie Railroad, 1869–1969.* San Marino, Calif.: Golden West Books, 1969.

Bezilla, Michael. *Electric Traction on the Pennsylvania Railroad, 1895–1968.* University Park, Pa.: Pennsylvania State University Press, 1980.

Brignano, Mary, and Hax McCullough. *The Search for Safety: A History of Railroad Signals and the People Who Made Them.* Pittsburgh: Union Switch & Signal Division, American Standard Inc., 1981.

Brown, John K. *The Baldwin Locomotive Works, 1888–1915: A Study in American Industrial Practice.* Baltimore: Johns Hopkins University Press, 1995.

Burgess, George H., and Miles C. Kennedy. *Centennial History of the Pennsylvania Railroad, 1846–1946.* Pennsylvania Railroad Co., 1949.

Cupper, Dan. *Crossroads of Commerce: The Pennsylvania Railroad Calendar Art of Grif Teller.* Richmond, Vt.: Great Eastern Publishing, 1992.

———. *Horseshoe Heritage: The Story of a Great Railroad Landmark.* Halifax, Pa.: Withers Publishing, 1993.

Daughen, Joseph R., and Peter Binzen. *The Wreck of the Penn Central.* Boston and Toronto: Little, Brown and Co., 1971.

Eagleson, Mike. *Steam on the Anthracite Roads.* New York: Quadrant Press, 1974.

Grant, H. Roger. *Erie Lackawanna: Death of an American Railroad, 1938–1992.* Stanford, Calif.: Stanford University Press, 1994.

Helmer, William F. *O. & W.: The Long Life and Slow Death of the New York, Ontario & Western Railway.* Berkeley, Calif.: Howell-North, 1959.

Hilton, George W. *The Ma & Pa: A History of the Maryland & Pennsylvania Railroad.* 2nd ed. Baltimore: Johns Hopkins University Press, 2000.

Holton, James L. *The Reading Railroad: History of a Coal Age Empire.* Vol. 1, *The Nineteenth Century.* Laury's Station, Pa: Garrigues House Publishers, 1989.

———. *The Reading Railroad: History of a Coal Age Empire.* Vol. 2, *The Twentieth Century.* Laury's Station, Pa: Garrigues House Publishers, 1992.

Hungerford, Edward. *Men of Erie: A Story of Human Effort.* New York: Random House, 1946.

Kobus, Ken, and Jack Consoli. *The Pennsy in the Steel City: 150 Years of the Pennsylvania Railroad in Pittsburgh.* Upper Darby, Pa.: Pennsylvania Railroad Technical & Historical Society, 1997.

Kulp, Randolph L., ed. *Railroads in the Lehigh River Valley.* Allentown, Pa.: Lehigh Valley Chapter, National Railway Historical Society, 1979.

McLean, Harold. *Pittsburgh & Lake Erie Railroad.* San Marino, Calif.: Golden West Books, 1980.

Pietrak, Paul. *Buffalo, Rochester & Pittsburgh Railway.* North Boston, N.Y.: Self-published, 1992.

Rainey, Lee, and Frank Kyper. *East Broad Top.* San Marino, Calif.: Golden West Books, 1982.

Rehor, John A. *The Nickel Plate Story.* Milwaukee, Wis.: Kalmbach Publishing Co., 1965.

Shaughnessy, Jim. *Delaware & Hudson.* Berkeley, Calif.: Howell-North Books, 1967.

Stover, John F. *History of the Baltimore & Ohio Railroad.* West Lafayette, Ind.: Purdue University, 1987.

Taber, Thomas T. *Delaware, Lackawanna & Western Railroad in the Nineteenth Century.* Muncy, Pa.: Thomas T. Taber III, 1977.

Taber, Thomas T., and Thomas T. Taber III. *Delaware, Lackawanna & Western Railroad in the Twentieth Century.* Muncy, Pa.: Thomas T. Taber III, 1980 .

Taber, Thomas T., III. *Railroads of Pennsylvania Encyclopedia and Atlas.* Muncy, Pa: Self-published, 1987.

Westhaeffer, Paul J. *History of the Cumberland Valley Railroad, 1835–1919.* Washington, D.C.: Washington, D.C., Chapter, National Railway Historical Society, 1979.